1812

*The War and
the World*

Attack on Fort McHenry (see pages 80-81)

1812

The War and the World

★ ★ ★ ★ ★ ★ ★ ★ ★ ★ ★ ★ ★ ★ ★ ★ ★ ★

BY WALTER BUEHR

Illustrated by the Author

RAND McNALLY & COMPANY

Chapter 1

As the first decade of the nineteenth century inscribed itself across the pages of history, the raw, weak new nation called the United States, consisting of only the thirteen original states, plus Vermont and Kentucky, straggled along the Atlantic Coast from Canada on the north to the border of Spanish-owned Florida on the south. This shallow fringe of settled land was all that lay beneath the Stars and Stripes. It was hemmed in on the west by the trackless Appalachian Mountains, beyond which lay a vast wilderness never seen by any white men except a few French voyageurs and they had been there over a hundred years earlier.

West of the mountains, from the southern shores of the Great Lakes, and extending westward to the Mississippi, lay wild hills and forests claimed by the original thirteen states as reserve territories, but still disputed by the British and by the Indians who lived there. These lands were just beginning to be thinly settled by American pioneer backwoodsmen and farmers.

To the south, all of Florida, which included a strip along the Gulf Coast westward to the mouth of the Mississippi, and all the lands west of the great river, right across the continent to the Pacific, were now owned by Spain. This southern territory had been hotly contested by the Spanish, French, and English for more than a hundred years and had often changed hands.

On the ninth of April, 1682, Robert Cavelier de La Salle and his party of explorers reached the mouth of the Mississippi from Canada, solemnly proclaimed all the land west of the great river the domain of King Louis of France, and named it Louisiana.

Frenchmen later also founded Mobile, Biloxi, and, in 1718,

New Orleans, but by the Treaty of Paris, at the end of the Seven Years War, France lost her vast territory of Louisiana, which was ceded to Spain, while England got the part of Louisiana east of the Mississippi and all of the Florida peninsula.

In 1769 Spanish troops thereupon had moved into New Orleans and closed the mouth of the big river to American and British shipping and trade. This was a serious blow to the upriver frontier farmers, who could get their crops to market only by

Mississippi flatboat

floating them down the Mississippi in flatboats to New Orleans, where they could be transferred to ocean-going ships.

The Spanish embargo would sooner or later have brought on a war, but before this happened, Spain, in another treaty in 1783, got Florida back and, by still another treaty, returned Louisiana to France.

That tiny part of the continent under the Stars and Stripes in 1800, had a population of only 5,308,000. Virginia, the Carolinas, and Georgia were agricultural states whose inhabitants lived by raising tobacco, cotton, and indigo for export, while the people of the northern states, where poor soil and a cold climate made farming unprofitable, became shipbuilders, seamen, fishermen, and merchants. Their interests were quite different from those of the plantation owners and farmers of the South, so the merchants, bankers, and ship owners of New England, who wanted a strong central government, backed the Federalist party, while the Southerners followed Thomas Jefferson and the Democratic party, which stood for less power in the federal government at Washington and greater states' rights.

New England, after the Revolution, was exhausted by seven long years of war. Everybody was broke, and the money issued by the federal government during and just after the war—the Continental bills derisively called "shinplasters"—was so worthless that the term "not worth a Continental" was often heard. In 1780, during the darkest part of the war, it took forty paper dollars to equal one gold dollar.

Still, New England, poor though she was, had dozens of good harbors, endless forests of straight pine timber, and thousands of skillful ship's carpenters and seamen, so naturally she turned to the sea for a living. For years the sound of the ax, the saw, and the calking mallet were seldom stilled in the shipyards beside every river and harbor in Maine, Massachusetts, and Connecticut, and a steady stream of square-rigged ships—barks and brigs, as well as schooners and sloops—slid down the ways into the cold Atlantic waters to seek their fortunes as merchantmen or fishermen.

Soon the Georges Banks and the Grand Banks were dotted

with the dories from American fishing schooners, and the Stars and Stripes were snapping from the mastheads of merchantmen in the harbors of Calcutta and Bombay, Capetown and Canton, Copenhagen and Liverpool. By 1793 American tonnage was greater than that of any other nation except England.

In 1794 war broke out between England and the government of revolutionary France, which had executed its king and become a republic, an action looked on with horror by every monarch and royal government in Europe. The warships of France and England began confiscating every merchantman belonging to the enemy they could catch, so that for some time the lion's share of the shipping trade fell to American ship owners whose vessels were the only neutral ships available to carry the world's freight safely. Only for a while. Then the two great powers blockaded each other's ports and refused to allow neutral ships to enter, so American merchantmen, denied European harbors, had to range farther afield.

Boston ships specialized in trade with India, sailing by way of Cape Horn and the Pacific Northwest, where they picked up cargoes of rich furs much prized by Orientals and traded them for coffee, spices, and tableware at Calcutta, Bombay, Rangoon, and the Celebes. Salem vessels rounded the Cape of Good Hope at the tip of Africa, crossed the Indian Ocean and the South China Sea to anchor in front of the godowns, or warehouses, of Canton, China, where they loaded tea, silks, spices, and chinaware to be sold in American and European markets.

By 1795, far-ranging Yankee ships—which had passed through the Strait of Gibraltar into the Mediterranean to trade with Italian, Greek, and Turkish merchants—began to run into serious trouble. The sultans and beys of the Arab states along the North African shores of the Mediterranean—Morocco, Algeria, Tunis, and Libya—had long preyed on all undefended shipping plying those waters, and even frequently raided French, Spanish, and Italian coastal towns across the Mediterranean. Their swift pirate

New England shipyard

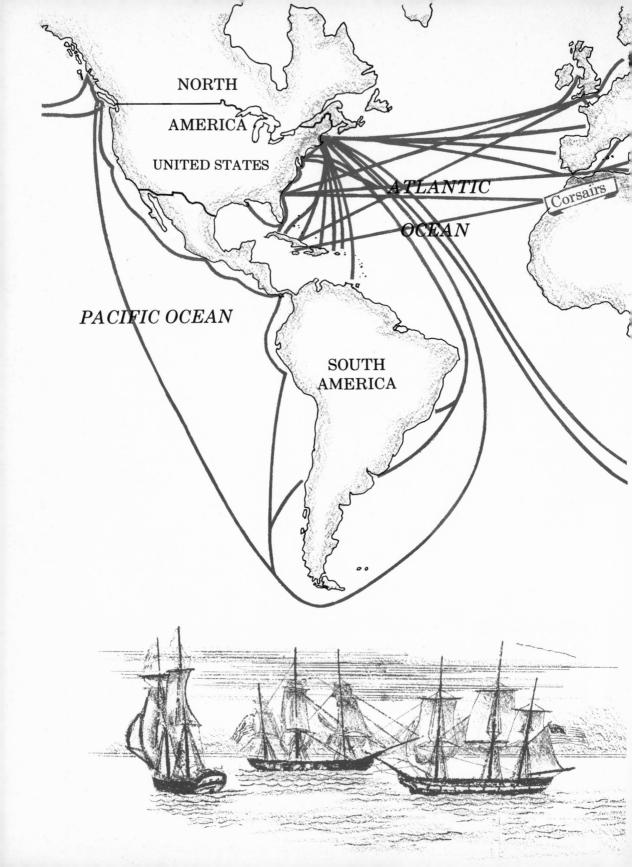

NORTH

AMERICA

UNITED STATES

ATLANTIC

OCEAN

Corsairs

PACIFIC OCEAN

SOUTH
AMERICA

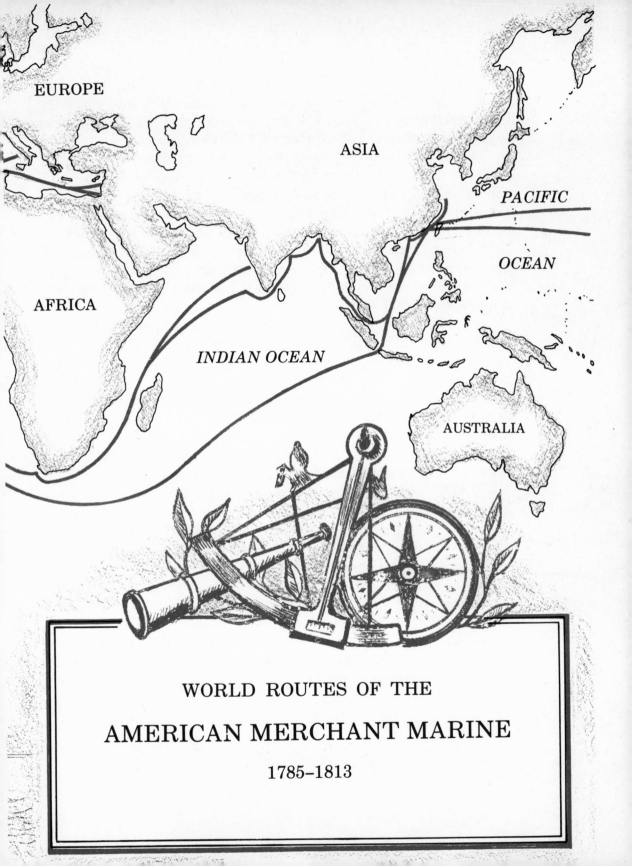

EUROPE

ASIA

PACIFIC

OCEAN

AFRICA

INDIAN OCEAN

AUSTRALIA

WORLD ROUTES OF THE

AMERICAN MERCHANT MARINE

1785–1813

craft, heavily armed and manned by crews of bloodthirsty cut-throats, captured helpless merchantmen, took them into the Barbary harbors, confiscated their cargoes and either killed the crews, sold them as slaves, or held them for heavy ransoms.

For a few years the American government, like many others, paid an annual tribute to the pirates to spare its ships, but by 1803, tired of paying blackmail, it sent Commodore Preble in command of a fleet of warships to attack the pirates' strongholds. He placed Captain Bainbridge at the head of an expedition to besiege Tripoli, but during the attack, his frigate, *Philadelphia*, grounded just outside the harbor. Bainbridge and his crew tried to scuttle the ship before the Tripolitans boarded her and captured them, but she was floated off and taken into the harbor, a prize.

Realizing that it would be too dangerous to permit *Philadelphia*, a powerful warship, to remain in the hands of the pirates, Preble assigned Stephen Decatur to lead a bold sally into the harbor in the very midst of the enemy fleet, to destroy the captured American frigate. In a captured Tripolitan ketch, the bold and desperate crew crept into the harbor, outwitted the guard ships, stormed aboard *Philadelphia*, and set her afire. Decatur and his men escaped in a small boat, while the enraged bey of Tripoli refused all suggestions of peace talks.

Preble then opened an attack on the port, led by the famous frigate *Constitution*, in which much damage was done to the forts of Tripoli, but the city remained unconquered. Preble was succeeded by Captain Samuel Barron, and a combined sea and land attack was planned, but before it started the bey, alarmed at the increasing strength of the American fleet, joined the other Barbary states in an uneasy peace agreement which was soon ignored. Not until the War of 1812 was over, and England and the United States were able to spare enough warships to force the Barbary pirates to surrender, was the Mediterranean freed from the constant terror of these corsairs.

Chapter 2

Events in France—our ally in the American Revolution—during the late eighteenth century, had a profound effect on what happened to the United States then, and in the early nineteenth century.

When the great Sun King, Louis XIV, died in 1715, his extravagances left France with a national debt sixteen times the nation's annual income. The government was decayed and corrupt, and taxes were unbearably burdensome, especially to the peasants and the very poor. Four-hundred thousand idle noblemen were supported extravagantly in their elegant chateaux or at the Court of Versailles by taxes wrung from the people, while the nobles paid none themselves and produced nothing of value. A clergy of one-hundred-forty thousand priests, monks, and nuns also paid no taxes while receiving an income of ninety million pounds a year paid from the nation's taxes.

The extravagance of the court and the corruption of the government continued through the reign of Louis XV. When Louis XVI ascended the throne, conditions had not improved, but the French people, who had witnessed the overthrow of British tyranny and the triumph of democracy in America (with the aid of French soldiers and sailors), longed for some of this freedom and equality for themselves. At last the dam of repression broke. In 1789 mobs attacked the Bastille—a fortress prison in Paris—and the King was dragged back to the city from his palace at Versailles a few miles away, by the National Guard. He was finally beheaded on January 21, 1793 and France became a republic, ruled by the National Convention. Soon the Reign of Terror began, led by Robespierre at the

Storming the Bastille

head of the Jacobins, in which thousands of Frenchmen were beheaded. His wild excesses finally caused the Convention to act, and
Robespierre was executed in July, 1794. With the Terror over, a
two-house legislature was organized, while the country was ruled
by a group of men called the Directory.

After the fall of the monarchy, a young Corsican artillery officer named Napoleon Bonaparte was rising rapidly in the Directory's army, because of the brilliant part he played in the defense of the republic against royal armies of other nations bent on destroying it. Napoleon soon changed from defense to offense, which resulted in a devastating war that killed off an entire generation of young men all over Europe, lasted for twenty-three years, and ended finally with the Battle of Waterloo. But that came later.

By 1796 Napoleon had been put in command of the Army of Italy, after which he conquered Venice and northern Italy and gained control of much other territory. In 1798 he was appointed commander of the Army of the East and sailed at the head of a great expeditionary force for the eastern Mediterranean, where he landed his troops in Egypt and captured Cairo. His brilliant successes on land were overshadowed at sea, where he met his first serious defeat at the hands of the British fleet under Lord Nelson, which utterly destroyed the French fleet at Aboukir Bay, cutting off the French expeditionary army in Egypt from home, supplies, munitions, and reinforcements.

Napoleon's dreams of a great eastern empire which would drive the British from India were blasted, so he deserted his army and slipped through the British blockade. He returned to France, where, in 1799, backed by the army, he overthrew the Directory. Power was then placed in the hands of three men called Consuls, with Napoleon as First Consul.

A short peace from 1802 to 1803 was soon broken, the two antagonists were at war again, and Napoleon was making elaborate plans to invade England with an army of two-hundred thousand trained veterans in thousands of small boats assembled all along the French Channel coast. He found that the French fleet was not up to the task of protecting his boats from the formidable British Channel fleet and heavy storms damaged many of his small craft, so, reluctantly, he had to call off his invasion.

This setback plus the disastrous French naval defeat at Trafalgar, off the coast of Spain, by Nelson's ships, put an end to Napoleon's dream of invading England and making her another

Other European armies were encumbered with unwieldy baggage trains

satellite. He realized at last that he could never hope to conquer England at sea; from now on he conceded that England would be the undisputed ruler of the ocean while he would be master of war on land.

Napoleon's troops were unequalled; other European armies were encumbered with great, unwieldy baggage trains of clumsy wagons that slowed the march. Their infantry wore heavy, awkward uniforms, carried mountainous packs, and marched in stiff parade formation. The French traveled light, carried little baggage, lived off the country, and made swift, incredibly long marches to appear before startled unprepared enemy armies and overwhelm them. Napoleon's cavalry was used with great skill and his artillery was far superior to the enemy's.

Only in two details were Napoleon's armies inferior. It was fortunate that they were accustomed to living off the country; otherwise they would often have gone hungry, because the French service of supply was very bad. French soldiers often wore rags and sometimes walked barefoot. The other failure was the medical service: though medical science was still very primitive in 1800, a wounded French soldier seldom received even that rough-and-ready care. For a generation after the wars, France was filled with crippled, armless or legless veterans, the wreckage of twenty years of continual fighting.

Napoleon's enormous ambition had encompassed a great new French empire on the American Continent with Louisiana its cen-

Napoleon's soldiers often wore rags

ter and New Orleans the capital. As a first step in this plan he had already revived slavery in the French West Indian Islands and had forbidden trade with any country except France, although the fierce and bloody resistance of the Haitians finally lost France that island.

The reopening of hostilities with England made Napoleon abandon that ambitious plan, fearing that if he kept Louisiana the stronger British navy would wrest it from him, annex it to its Canadian colony, and so become too powerful in America ever to be defeated there.

To keep Louisiana out of British hands, Napoleon agreed to sell it to the United States; also he needed money to carry on his continual warfare. The Americans, fearing that if Napoleon defeated England he might establish a western empire next door to them, which indeed he had planned to do, gladly accepted the offer.

After some haggling, a price of fifteen million dollars was agreed upon, surely one of the greatest real estate bargains of all time. On December 20, 1803, Governor Claiborne formally took possession of Louisiana, in one swoop increasing the territory of the United States by 140 percent, securing its western boundaries and gaining complete control of the Mississippi from its source to its mouth.

Control of the Mississippi would soon become especially important to the Middle West, for in 1812 the first steamboat puffed up the Mississippi. No longer was river traffic only one way—downstream, with the current, in flatboats. Steamers now could travel to St. Louis and far up the Mississippi and the Missouri, carrying passengers and freight at a time when there were neither good roads nor railroads.

Meanwhile in France, on December 2, 1804, Napoleon took the final step in his grandiose ambitions. He placed a crown on his own head and declared himself Emperor Napoleon I. Prevented from carrying on naval operations by Nelson's victory over the French and Spanish fleets at Trafalgar, Napoleon now concentrated on land campaigns, raised an army of a million men in France alone, and made himself master of all Europe.

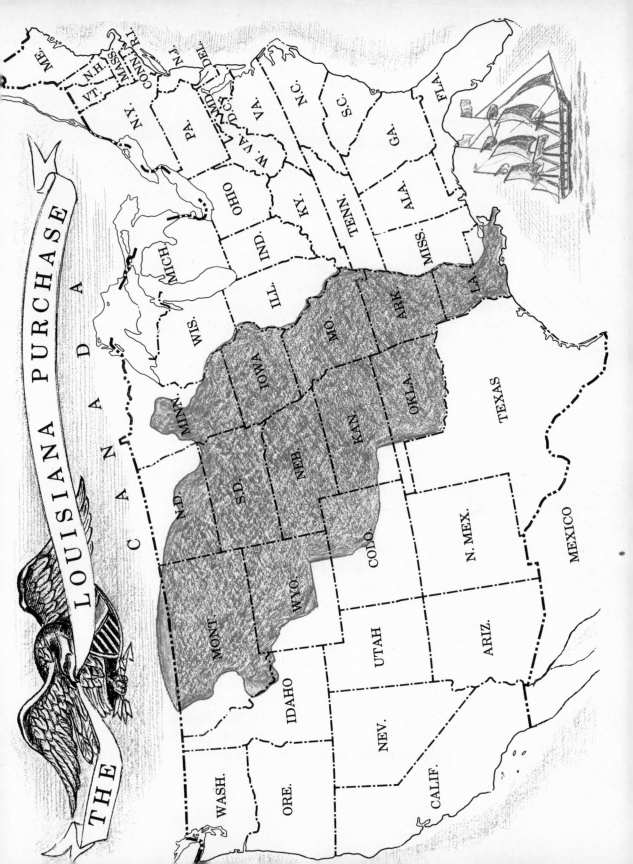

THE LOUISIANA PURCHASE

Chapter 3

Across the Atlantic in the United States, President Jefferson was determined to consolidate the gains in territory made by the Louisiana Purchase. Although this had more than doubled the area of the nation, in the year 1803 most of it had never even been seen by a white man.

A few small Spanish military posts dotted the Southwest and, many years before, French voyageurs coming down from Canada had paddled down the great Mississippi to the Gulf of Mexico. A few American trappers had paddled up the big rivers for short distances after beaver, but beyond that nobody in Washington, New York, Boston, or anywhere along the Atlantic seaboard had the slightest idea of what this vast territory contained.

Tales of great rivers, swarming with beaver, flowing out of a towering snowcapped range far to the west (called the Great Rock Mountains by the Indians), of dense forests and vast prairies dark with thundering herds of buffalo, were brought back by the trappers, but nobody knew for certain what lay between the Mississippi and the mouth of the Columbia River on the far-off Pacific coast, which had been discovered by Robert Gray in 1792, in his little ship *Columbia*.

President Jefferson believed that exploration might reveal that the headwaters of the east-flowing Missouri River and the west-flowing Columbia, both originating in those Rock Mountains we now call the Rockies, might be close enough together so that a water route from the Mississippi to the Pacific might be established with only one portage between the two sources in the mountains. This would open up the entire vast new land to fur trapping and would encourage settlers to move west and establish farms.

First of all, this new land had to be traversed by an expedition headed by men who could map it, observe the animals, plants, geology, and geography and bring back complete scientific reports on what they saw. The President chose two young army officers, Meriwether Lewis and William Clark, to lead the expedition. When they reached St. Louis in December, 1803, they found trouble. Because the Spanish commander of the army post at St. Louis had not yet been informed of the transfer of Louisiana to France from Spain by the treaty of San Ildefonso in 1802, and its subsequent sale to the United States, he refused to let the expedition pass, and they had to winter along the river a few miles from the post.

During the winter, while waiting for permission to go on, they built several boats in which to make the trip upstream, purchased weapons, instruments, and supplies, as well as trade goods to barter with the redskins, and worked out their plans.

Then in March, 1804, they got action! The Spanish commander got orders to turn Louisiana over to France, and hauled down his flag, which was replaced by the French tricolor, but the French knew of the sale to the United States, so on that same day they lowered their flag, and the Stars and Stripes floated proudly from the post flagstaff. St. Louis was under three flags in one day!

Now the way was open. Lewis and Clark cast off their boats and, on May 14, started up the Missouri on their five-thousand mile continent-spanning exploration. Along the way they met many generally friendly Indian tribes, to whom they gave presents of knives, hatchets, and trinkets and told of their new great white chief in Washington. Along the way they saw huge numbers of deer, elk, bear, beaver, and buffalo, as well as ducks, geese, quail, and passenger pigeons. There was so much fresh meat that the men gorged themselves and had enough left to jerk strips of it to cure in the sun for emergencies.

In November they arrived at the mouth of the Knife River in the Mandan country in the Dakotas, where they went into camp for the next winter. The party, which now consisted of twenty-seven men, Sacajawea, an Indian woman (who became their interpreter), and her baby, started out again in dugout canoes on April

The Lewis and Clark expedition

7, 1805. Lewis and Clark sent the rest of the expedition back in the larger boats to St. Louis, because these were too large to navigate the upper reaches of the river. When they reached the headwaters, they met their first western Indians, with whom Sacajawea, a western Indian herself, could converse. From these Shoshones they bought horses, made pack saddles from boat oars, loaded their baggage on them, and started across the mountains over the Continental Divide, after hiding their canoes.

On October 5, they reached the Snake River, where they built more canoes and floated down into the great Columbia. There they saw, along the banks, many villages of the Flathead tribe, which existed almost entirely on the salmon that came up the river from the sea to spawn every spring.

Early in November, after surviving the Great Falls and the Cascades of the Columbia, they floated into a wide bay and got their first glimpse of the Pacific. On a wooded height along a creek they built a log stockade, which they called Fort Clatsop, where they prepared to winter again.

Although the Indians told them that ships often came into the bay, Lewis and Clark never saw a single vessel while they camped on the coast, which was a bitter disappointment. They had planned to replenish their supplies and trade goods from a ship they had expected Jefferson to send, or from some trading vessel, but by early spring they abandoned hope of seeing a ship. On April 6, 1806, they started back up the Columbia, over the Rockies, and down the Missouri, arriving safely at St. Louis on September 23, 1806. On the entire trip only one man, who died of a burst appendix, was lost.

Lewis and Clark and their party were the first white men to cross the continent, and their reports on the geography, the Indians, the animals, birds, and plant life were of tremendous importance to the President and to the government, as well as to the trappers and pioneers and, later, to the Oregon settlers and the '49ers (the California gold seekers). Their explorations were the first steps in the westward tide of emigration which was already beginning, while, east of the Mississippi, the nation was challenging the might of the British navy and parrying military thrusts by British regulars from Canada.

Chapter 4

As the war between England and France grew hotter, the threat to American ships and sailors became greater. Each side tried to prevent the flow of goods to enemy ports, but to England this was much more vital than to France. A small island kingdom, she depended for her very existence upon her trade with her colonial empire. She had to keep sea lanes open or starve, so her warships had not only to be ready to fight French war vessels whenever they ventured to sea, but they also had to protect their own convoys of merchantmen from enemy raiders. At the end of the eighteenth century England had lost her American colonies, but she still had two very profitable sources of wealth overseas. Most of the Lesser Antilles—those West Indian islands lying south and east of Cuba, Hispaniola, and Puerto Rico—were in British hands.

In the early 1800's most of the world's sugar and tobacco were grown on French or English West Indian plantations with slave labor. Only ships flying the flag of the nation owning the island were permitted to anchor there and load or unload. These monopolies were so immensely valuable that the islands were bitterly fought over by the British and French, and changed hands frequently, as first one and then the other fleet got the upper hand. Nowadays, because sugar can be grown in many places, and cane sugar must share the market with sugar beets, the West Indies are generally very poor, with only the tourist trade and some banana and pineapple plantations to save them. At the beginning of the nineteenth century, hundreds of sugar-, molasses-, and rum-laden merchantmen traversed the Caribbean and Atlantic in great guarded convoys, while enemy warships and privateers snapped at the heels of any merchant ship that strayed too far.

England's second source of wealth was in the East. Here, on the other side of the world, the British East India Company, a private trading venture which had traded with the East Indies and India in a small way, had gradually expanded until it had become the actual political power over the maharajas and princes of all the various Indian states making up the entire subcontinent, with a monopoly of all trade. This lasted until the British government took control in 1803, abolishing the power of the British East India Company.

While it was in power the British East India Company, known at that time as the "John Company," for some strange reason, had its own army and operated vast fleets of ponderous, well-armed merchantmen under its own flag, which sailed from Bombay and Calcutta across the Indian Ocean, around the tip of Africa, and then north to British ports. The cargoes they carried in both directions brought such large profits that the captain of an Indiaman, who got a share of the profits of each cargo, could retire after a few voyages, but these rich rewards also attracted many privateers and pirates, so the convoys had to be escorted by British warships all along the ten-thousand-mile route.

The British navy was terribly strained to fulfill all the many tasks imposed on it, and its ships were constantly short of crews. One reason for this was the harsh, sometimes brutal treatment of the sailors, who were often punished by hanging or ferocious flogging for even minor infractions. Another reason was the heavy labor, poor food, and unhealthy, miserable living conditions aboard His Majesty's ships, the low pay and the long enlistments, during which the crews often spent years afloat without ever being allowed to go ashore even to see their families, for fear of desertion. On top of this was the constant threat of being crippled for life or dying an agonizing death after an enemy broadside.

Few men, therefore, enlisted voluntarily, so most of them were dragged from jails or debtors' prisons or seized in the streets and grogshops of coastal towns by naval press-gangs (short for impress). They were driven aboard without notice to their families, and forced to sign on against their will. Men deserted if they thought they had the slightest chance of escape (to be caught meant hang-

ing), and a good many got their release by dying aboard from sickness or wounds.

British warships had to carry very large crews to handle sail, man the guns, fill the gaps left by disabled men and deserters, and to supply prize crews to bring captured enemy merchantmen or warships into British ports. A strange custom of the British navy made each ship's captain responsible for keeping a full crew aboard; he could lose his command for failure to do so. Any post captain, whose press-gangs were unable to find enough men ashore, had a right to stop any British merchant vessel he met, send a lieutenant and armed boat's crew aboard, and seize as many of the crew as he needed to fill out his quarter bills (list of watches). When British ships no longer were able to supply enough men, the next step was to stop foreign ships and search them for British deserters, at which time a seaman had to prove to the boarding officer's satisfaction that he *wasn't* British.

As the war with France wore on, the British navy's need for men grew more desperate, and its cruisers began taking American-born seamen as well as British deserters from American ships.

The high-handed search and impressment tactics came to a head in 1807. A new United States frigate, *Chesapeake*, sailed out of Chesapeake Bay on a shakedown cruise, with her guns still unmounted and unprepared to fight. The British cruiser *Leopard* intercepted her and demanded the right to put a boarding party aboard to search for British deserters. When the American captain refused, *Leopard* opened fire, killing some of the crew and forcing *Chesapeake* to submit to search. American war fever ran high after this insult, but President Jefferson did his best to find a peaceful solution. This interception of unarmed American ships continued for years, right up to the War of 1812, and Britain's refusal to abandon it was one of the main causes leading to the declaration of war in 1812.

The second principal cause was the refusal of Britain (and

Press-gangs at work

New England harbor after Jefferson's embargo

France, too) to recognize the neutrality of American merchant ships, which were forbidden by the British to trade in French ports, and by the French to enter British home or colonial ports. However, since the British had many more cruisers at sea than the French, their interference was much greater and caused the Americans more resentment.

President Jefferson realized that war was becoming more and more likely, so, to avoid giving the British or French any excuse to open hostilities against us, he decided in 1807 to declare an embargo which would forbid all commerce between the United States and England or France, in the hope that the loss of so much trade would make British merchants demand that American rights be respected.

The embargo was in force throughout Jefferson's term of office and into Madison's, but it failed to achieve its purpose. However, it did succeed in ruining the port cities of New England. Merchants and shipping men went bankrupt, captains and seamen were jobless on the beach, and ships lay rotting at deserted docks. Such bitter resentment rose against President Madison's government that many New Englanders were in favor of seceding from the United States and making a separate peace with England.

The embargo did bring about one good result, though. Prevented from following their normal pursuit—the sea—the Yankees had to find other ways of earning a living, and many turned to small manufacturing which, in the end, led to an industrial New England and greater prosperity than shipping could have given it.

At the opening of the nineteenth century, there had been bitter wrangling among the different parts of the new nation. The growing population in the newly opened lands across the Appalachian Mountains wanted war with England because British fur traders interfered with American trappers and because American frontiersmen believed that the British were inciting the Indians to attack and murder the settlers and burn their homes. They wanted the British driven from Canada, which they would have liked to see annexed to the United States.

The people of New England, on the other hand, were strongly against war with Britain. The unworkable embargo had at last been repealed on March 1, 1809, and the inhabitants of the port cities wanted to continue trading with England and the West Indies. By this time Easterners were growing suspicious of the French, their former allies. Americans had at first approved of the French Revolution; they were happy to see a European country throw off the shackles of the corrupt monarchists and follow the American example toward democracy. Lately, though, the French government seemed to be growing more and more aggressive, and Easterners began to feel that England was perhaps the lesser evil.

The feelings of the New Englanders were well-known in England, where a good many people were sympathetic to the Americans, even though King George III and his ministers were not. However, the anti-British sentiment in the South and West grew too strong to resist, and Congress finally declared war on England on June 18, 1812, just five days before the British Parliament revoked its Orders in Council prohibiting American ships from trading in European and West Indian ports (one of the main reasons for the declaration), although it still refused to stop the impressment of sailors from American ships.

Chapter **5**

Despite the destructive wars throughout the world, during the last part of the eighteenth century great progress was being made in the humanities, in the fields of science and invention, and in exploration.

The year 1791 saw the abolition of slavery in France, although it was not until 1807 that the slave trade in English territories was abolished.

The steam engine, developed by James Watt in 1769, pumped water from flooded coal mines, ran railroads and ships, and ran the power machines which made the tools that lightened the labors of farmers and workmen in town and country. The application of waterwheels and steam engines to power machines would soon introduce the Industrial Revolution, which would have a greater influence on people everywhere than all the revolutions and wars.

The first experiments in that wonder worker, electricity, were beginning to bear fruit. Benjamin Franklin conducted his famous kite experiment in 1752; Galvani and Volta later developed this mysterious force further along to its twentieth-century triumphs.

In 1785 Valentin Haüy, also a Frenchman, began printing the first books with raised characters for the blind, and in 1798, another Frenchman, Robert, invented a paper-making machine which made it possible for everybody to afford books and newspapers.

From 1771 to 1778 the earliest explorations of the Canadian Arctic took place, and, in 1773, Captain James Cook was first to cross the Antarctic Circle.

In 1793 the cotton gin was invented by Eli Whitney, a young Yankee, assuring cotton mills a plentiful supply of cheap cotton,

Eli Whitney's cotton gin

free of seeds, which before this had to be combed out slowly and expensively by hand. The cotton gin, together with the earlier fly shuttle (1738), the spinning jenny (1767), and the power loom (1785) finally made it possible to produce cheap, good-quality cloth. No longer would fibers have to be twisted into thread with distaff and spindle or a spinning wheel, and the cloth be woven on a hand-operated cottage loom. Nor would plows and shovels and cooking pots be hammered into shape on an anvil in a blacksmith shop. Machines would soon take over most of the world's production.

In 1794 the first telegraph, a manually operated semaphore system, was invented and connected Paris with Lille. Under Napoleon, who saw its military possibilities, it was greatly extended and was used constantly during his campaigns.

Perhaps the most important work of the eighteenth century to benefit humanity was in the field of medicine. Experiment, research, and discovery were piercing the veil of ignorance and superstition which had held back medicine for centuries, laying the groundwork for future important discoveries.

In England the study of anatomy was much advanced by the Hunter brothers, William and John, at their famous anatomic theater and museum, built in London in 1770. John Hunter was also responsible for making surgery respectable, and a recognized branch of scientific medicine, instead of the barbarous methods, often carried on by barbers as a sideline, used in the past.

At last, in the eighteenth century, a connection was recognized between filth and disease. Between 1777 and 1788 Johann Peter Frank published, in Germany, a four-volume work that laid the foundation for modern public hygiene.

Eight years later, in 1796, vaccination against smallpox, the great scourge of the eighteenth century, was discovered by Dr. Jenner, an Englishman.

However, in the fields of transportation and communication, not much progress had been made toward the "one world" we know today. On land, travelers still had to walk, ride horseback, or

Manually operated semaphore system

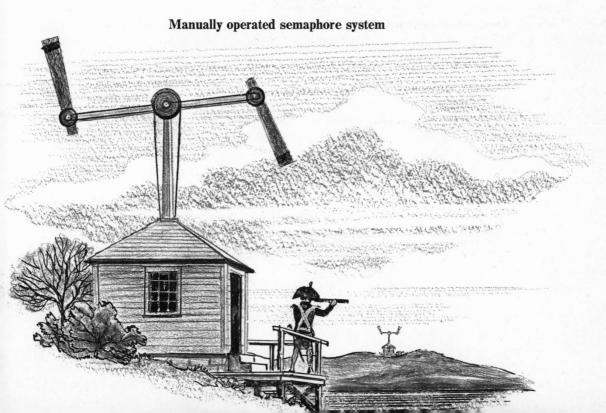

Bedroom of posting inn

sit in jolting wagons or coaches, over roads that were not even as good as the Roman roads built two centuries before Christ. The distance a land traveler could cover in a day was always limited by the speed of a horse. It took about six weeks to go from Boston to Philadelphia; much longer in winter or in muddy weather. The traveler spent his nights in the rough-and-ready posting inns, in dirty, unheated, candle-lit bedrooms, in which signs admonished him to remove his boots before going to bed, and forbade more than six occupants to a bed. Only fireplaces heated the downstairs public rooms, and if the fire went out, it took a brisk fifteen-minute work-out to rekindle it with flint and steel and tinder; the sulphur match was not invented until 1836.

Stephenson's steam locomotive, which pulled several carriages behind it on rails, made its appearance in England in 1814, but rail-roads would not supplant the stagecoach for another forty years.

At sea, traveling was slightly more comfortable and, with favorable winds, faster, too. But the packet ship still had to depend on those fickle winds, just as the Greeks did in the seventh century B.C., and Columbus did also in the *Santa María* in 1492.

John Fitch, in Philadelphia, in 1789, and Robert Fulton, in

New York, in 1807, had designed and built ships whose paddle wheels were turned by a steam engine, but not until 1819 did the first steamship, *Savannah*, cross the Atlantic, and she soon ran out of wood for her boiler and had to make most of the trip under canvas.

The speed of communication was limited at sea by the sailing ship and on land by the mail coach or express rider, except for Napoleon's semaphore telegraph which was, however, useless in fog or rain (the semaphores did have lanterns at night). Not until 1843 was distance conquered by Samuel Morse's electric telegraph, and fifteen years more would pass before Europe and America were linked by the Atlantic cable.

John Fitch's paddle-wheel ship with steam engine

Chapter 6

When Congress declared war on England, the weak, young United States was defying the greatest sea power in the world. In 1812 Britain had 119 first-rate (ships of 100 guns or more) and second-rate (74 to 90 guns) ships-of-the-line, 245 50-gun ships and 32–38 gun frigates, besides several hundred smaller brigs, sloops, schooners, and cutters. Her shipyards were busy with a big building program, and her iron foundries were turning out large numbers of cannon of all calibers. One out of every two hundred inhabitants of the British Isles was serving in the Royal Navy.

The American government, realizing that it had no chance of matching the power of the enormously strong British navy on the high seas, decided not to build any large warships in 1812, but to concentrate on a large number of very small gunboats, each carrying just one gun, to be used only to defend rivers and harbors. They proved to be a dismal failure; they had to anchor before firing their guns, for fear of capsizing. They were never of the slightest use during the war; only afterward, at the Battle of New Orleans, were they put to good use.

This left the country with a tiny navy, consisting of vessels built after the Revolution, before the gunboat decision. There were three 44-gun frigates, authorized by Congress before 1793 and designed by the famous naval architect, Joshua Humphreys of Philadelphia. Since the United States was too poor to challenge the British with heavy three-deckers, Humphreys decided to design a class of frigates more powerful than those of any other nation, but fast enough to out-sail and escape from more powerful ships or enemy squadrons. They were the famous *Constitution*, *President*, and *United States*, and were to prove enormously successful against British frigates during the whole of the War of 1812.

The keel of *Constitution*, the best known and the greatest fighter of the three, was laid in 1794 and she slid down the ways on October 21, 1797. She was a full-rigged ship, 175 feet long, with a beam of 43½ feet, and she was a fast sailer, at times logging a speed of better than 15 land miles an hour. Rated at 44 guns, she carried at different times, according to her captain's wishes, from 38 to 55 guns, more when some of them were carronades—lighter weight large-caliber guns with a short range.

The navy also had four smaller frigates of from 32 to 38 guns—*Chesapeake*, *Congress*, *Constellation*, and *Essex*—one corvette—*Adams*, 28 guns—two ship-rigged sloops—*Wasp* and *Hornet*, each 18 guns—and six brigs of 12, 14, and 16 guns, which were slow and poor sailers.

The inequality between the tiny American fleet and the much stronger British fleet was not quite as marked as might appear. The British fleet had to blockade every French and Spanish port in the Atlantic and Mediterranean to keep the enemy vessels from getting to sea to wreak havoc on British convoys of merchantmen. It had to keep a supply line open to British armies in Portugal and Spain, escorting convoys loaded with supplies for the armies. It also had to keep an eye on the British West Indian Islands against French attacks on her shipping there, and also convoy cargo-laden English ships from the islands across the Atlantic and protect them from cruisers and privateers.

Besides, she was trying to blockade the long American coast. To reach a station off Boston, New York, or the Chesapeake, British frigates had to make the long voyage across the Atlantic from England, or at least from their base at Halifax, Nova Scotia, keeping constant watch in stormy weather and winter gales, always at sea until forced to return to Halifax for stores and water and refitting. At the beginning of the War of 1812, the hard-pressed British navy could spare only a few 74's and frigates to combat the Americans and blockade them.

Above: Ship rigged sloop-of-war; *Right:* 100-gun first rater

Above: Gun brig
Left: Frigate *U.S.S. Constitution*

74-gun third rater

Frigate-built corvette

In the summer of 1812, American Commodore John Rodgers, commanding a squadron of five ships—the frigates *President* and *United States*, the light frigate *Congress*, the brig *Argus*, and the sloop *Hornet*—was patrolling the coast from Long Island southward to prevent British cruisers from stopping American merchantmen. Rodgers' flagship was taking on stores in New York harbor when the declaration of war was announced in the city, and the Commodore put to sea within an hour, before orders from Washington to lay up his ship in harbor could reach and stop him.

Rodgers' squadron began patrolling shipping lanes to try to intercept and make prizes of British merchantmen bound to or from Jamaica and the other West Indian Islands. He soon encountered the British frigate *Belvidera*, but she managed to escape him and hurried to Halifax to report the declaration of war and the presence of an American squadron on the high seas.

While Rodgers made few prizes during the four wide sweeps across the Atlantic he carried on in the next two and a half years, he did succeed in giving the British Vice Admiral, Sawyer, in command of the Halifax station, plenty to worry about.

Admiral Sawyer would no longer dare to send out a single frigate to patrol a stretch of the coast where the American squadron might pounce on it at any time; he had always to keep enough of his ships together to be able to face the Americans if they should meet. This meant that he could cover only a small segment of the coast, leaving big gaps in his blockade for American merchantmen to slip through.

Sawyer's first squadron to patrol under the new conditions consisted of *Africa*, 64, and four frigates, under Captain Broke, which was cruising off the New Jersey coast when a strange sail was sighted. This was *Constitution*, bound from Annapolis—where Captain Isaac Hull had been signing on a new crew—to New York. Hull soon realized that the squadron bearing down on him was not Rodgers', but in fact a powerful enemy force, and he spread every stitch of canvas to escape it.

When he saw he was in for a long stern chase, Hull had a 24-pounder and a long 18 dragged aft and pointed astern through holes he had cut in the taffrail of the quarterdeck, and two more

24-pounders aimed through the stern windows of his cabin on the deck below. This would prevent the British from sending armed boats filled with boarding parties to overtake his ship if it was becalmed. A couple of whiffs of grapeshot or canister from those stern guns would soon discourage small boats.

The wind for the next two days varied from a dead calm to the lightest of breezes, with the leader of the pursuing Britishers just out of range astern of *Constitution*. It was a desperate situation for Captain Hull. If a fortunate breeze brought the British squadron within range, it was all up with the greatly out-gunned *Constitution*. Every trick of seamanship he knew would be needed for him to escape certain annihilation.

The ship's boats were launched and towing lines rigged from their sterns to the ship's bows. Relays of boat crews manned the oars and pulled feverishly to drag the great bulk of their ship ahead. It was exhausting work in the blinding sun during that blazing summer day, just to make her move at all. Worse, the Americans saw that the British ships were sending their boats to help the nearest Britisher, *Shannon*, and with all that extra manpower, she was gaining.

Captain Hull, in desperation, ordered the ten tons of drinking water in *Constitution*'s water casks pumped overboard to lighten his ship and gain a fraction more of speed. Then Charles Morris, Hull's first lieutenant, discovered that the ocean here was only one-hundred-fifty feet deep so that an anchor would find bottom, and he suggested kedging.

Quickly a kedge anchor (a light anchor with four sharp-pronged arms) was lowered to the ship's launch alongside and suspended from a strongback, a frame built out over the boat's stern. The anchor was made fast to several spliced cables coiled in the stern sheets of the boat, with the other end running back to *Constitution*'s capstan, the windlass used to bring up the anchor. Then the boat was rowed ahead until all the cable was paid out and the anchor was dropped to the bottom. All hands then fell to the capstan bars, winding the ship slowly forward toward the anchor buried in the mud. Meantime, another boat with another dangling anchor was sent ahead and, when the ship was hove to the first

anchor, the cable from the next anchor ahead was transferred to the capstan and the back-breaking toil was resumed.

The British couldn't copy this maneuver, because the boats carrying their anchors would have come within range of *Constitution*'s stern guns, which would have blown them to pieces.

All day this snail-like but deadly race continued. Sometimes, when a tiny cat's-paw of breeze sprang up, the boats were hastily hoisted aboard while topmen hauled buckets of water to the mast-head to spill over the sails. Wet canvas held the wind better than dry, but, unfortunately, the water evaporated so quickly in the heat that the sailwetting had to be continuous. As soon as the wind died, the boats were again lowered and the weary kedging continued.

The next morning the breeze had increased enough to bring in the boats again, and *Constitution* slowly gained on the enemy. At sunset a squall approached and Captain Hull had his light canvas furled and plain sails reefed, but, as soon as the worst of it passed, he shook out his reefs to make good eleven knots for a while, and finally outdistanced the British who were slower in sail handling.

By the next dawn, *Constitution* was almost out of sight and the British squadron gave up the chase, heading east to escort a British convoy from the West Indies, and leaving the American coast unblockaded by any British cruiser for seven weeks.

Constitution being towed by anchor

Chapter 7

The interruption of the blockade for almost two months was a godsend to the hundreds of ships of the American merchant marine, second in tonnage only to the British. United States vessels had been scattered all over the globe, from Russia, Holland, and Denmark to Mediterranean and West Indian ports, and as far as the East Indies, India, and China. Their home ports, however, were mostly along that short stretch of the American coast between Boston and Salem on the north, and Chesapeake Bay on the south.

Most of their captains had not yet heard of the state of war with England and so would have become easy prey to any blockading British cruisers. Had they been captured they would have been sent back to England as prizes, with staggering losses to New England merchants and shipowners. With the blockaders away most of them reached port safely, and instead of becoming British prizes, many of them were fitted out as privateers and instead went out to capture British merchantmen.

A good many owners of fast, well-built ships, attracted by the very high freight rates, became blockade-runners, while others armed their vessels with cannon and went after even richer, though riskier, rewards as privateers. A privateer was a privately owned merchant vessel fitted with cannon and given letters of marque by its own government, which permitted it to attack and capture, during wartime, any vessel it encountered which sailed under the flag of the enemy. As a sort of private warship, it put a prize crew aboard any enemy merchantman it could capture and sent it into the nearest friendly port, where ship and cargo were sold and the money given to the owners and crew of the privateer.

Not only did privateering bring in much-needed goods and money, but every capture reduced the enemy's strength. Of course, enemy cruisers, which were usually much stronger than the privateers, captured as many of them as they could and made the crews prisoners of war, but sometimes a privateer showed fight against a small enemy naval vessel and even came off winner in the battle.

The ocean soon swarmed with American privateers, and British shipping everywhere suffered such heavy losses that British

American privateer *Grand Turk* captures British packet *Hinchinbrook*

merchantmen had to travel in large convoys escorted by warships. Even then they were not always safe; American yards were turning out very fast, able privateers armed with long guns and carronades in their broadsides, plus a Long Tom (a long range cannon) mounted on a pivot on deck. Such a ship could cut out some luckless vessel at the other end of a long convoy from its lumbering 74 or frigate escort, give it a broadside, put aboard a prize crew, and escape with its prize before the warship could get near enough to fire.

True, there were some drawbacks to the war effort because of privateering; these ships were built and manned, not by pure patriots, but by men who expected to make a profit. The crews got much higher pay plus a share in any prize money, much more than the navy could offer, so that the navy found it difficult to sign on crews because so many of the skilled seamen had gone privateering. Also, privateers could not be ordered into battle to aid the navy; they usually avoided joining battle with stronger enemy forces.

During the greatest days of the American privateers in 1812, there were 526 of these armed ships, brigs, sloops, and schooners, some as powerful as naval sloops-of-war, mounting as many as 20 guns, sniffing along the trade routes for lone merchantmen, prowling along the flanks of huge convoys. They were ready to snap up any unwary merchantman that strayed too far from the protection of the navy escort, even sailing into the English Channel and along the coast of Britain, to take as prizes ships whose captains were foolish enough to leave their convoys and dash for their home ports when they approached England. Only 148 American privateers were captured by the British navy. The records show that during the War of 1812, prizes to the number of 1330, worth $39,000,000, were taken by privateer captains who, as former merchantmen themselves, knew the routes such ships would take at different times of the year, and understood the navigating habits of merchant captains better than did the naval officers, whose warships took only 670 prizes from Britain. So heavy were the losses of cargoes that the price of sugar and coffee rose over 100 percent in London in 1814.

Chapter 8

After that hair-raising escape from the British squadron, *Constitution* had made port safely in Boston, refilled her empty water butts, taken on stores, and put to sea again.

Just over the horizon, Captain James Dacres, commander of His Majesty's frigate *Guerrière*, proudly surveyed from his quarter-deck the lines of sleek black cannon below him, snugly secured in their taut breechings, behind closed gunports, against the rough seas which plunged the ship's stem into the foam up to her bowsprit. Captain Dacres, resplendent in a blue swallow-tailed brass-buttoned coat trimmed with gold lace and epaulets, white waistcoat, breeches and stockings, black pumps and a huge cocked hat, was very young for a Royal Navy post captain. The fact that he was the son of an admiral who had distinguished himself in the battles in the West Indies in 1807 certainly helped his career, but at twenty-eight he had already commanded warships for six years and had seen much active service.

The captain's bearing bespoke utter confidence; was he not commander of a ship of the Royal Navy which had outfought every other navy in Europe—the Spanish, the Dutch, the Danes, even Napoleon's imperial fleet? *Guerrière* had been captured from the French, who knew how to design better, faster vessels than the British shipyards could build. When she surrendered, she was armed with forty-nine guns, which she still mounted, although the British navy, to confuse the enemy, rated her as only a thirty-eight.

Captain Dacres was confident that she could conquer any-

Captain Dacres aboard *H.M.S. Guerrière*

thing near her size and outrun any larger battleship. He was sure he could handle any of the big American frigates; although they were more heavily built and had larger crews, they rated only forty-four guns, some rumored to be light-weight carronades.

Only a few days before this brisk, blowy August 19, 1812, *Guerrière* had been part of the squadron that had almost captured the American *Constitution*, but after a long, agonizing stern chase she had managed to give them the slip in a squall. Now he was heading for Halifax for a refit, stores, and water, and he hoped that when he resumed his station he might have the luck to come up with *Constitution* or another of those Yankee frigates and show them the invincibility of the Royal Navy.

Suddenly a sharp hail from a lookout in the crosstrees brought him to the rail, a brassbound telescope clapped to his eye. Now he could see the sun glinting on white topsails of a cut he thought he recognized. Soon he realized that this was indeed *Constitution*, which had escaped his squadron a few days ago; now she was heading straight for him, this time with the odds equal. Dacres might have turned tail and escaped from an enemy probably a bit more powerful than his ship, but no British commander would have dared avoid a fight with a single, closely matched adversary. From a big 74 or a squadron, yes, but to run away from another frigate would have ruined his career and forever disgraced him.

He ordered *Guerrière* cleared for action, sent down his royals (the topmost sails) and reduced to "fighting sails"—topsails and jib—then hove to, awaiting the enemy's approach. Presently Captain Dacres ordered a broadside fired, but the balls fell short, so he clapped on sail, steering the same course as the Yankee astern.

Sailing warships of that day carried most of their guns in broadsides, projecting from gunports in rows along the ships' sides, with only two to four guns facing forward or aft, because of lack of room in bow or stern. Therefore, the maximum effectiveness of the guns could be utilized only when the ship was turned broadside to the enemy, and the greatest damage could be done to him when a broadside was fired along the length of his ship, over either the bow or stern, dismounting guns and slaughtering many of the crew. This was known as "raking."

Dacres attempted this, yawing from time to time, so that his broadside would bear on the overtaking Yankee, with the hope of dismasting her or so damaging the rigging as to lose steerage way. Any sailing warship with masts or rigging destroyed would at once become a helpless hulk and the enemy could cross her bows or stern at will, raking her until her decks were a bloody confusion of splintered rails, overturned guns, and slaughtered crew, with never a chance to bring her own batteries to bear.

None of *Guerrière*'s broadsides or *Constitution*'s bow-chaser balls did much damage, so that after forty-five minutes the faster *Constitution* drew abreast and the frigates began exchanging furious broadsides for fifteen minutes. Battles between such sailing warships were usually decided in less than half an hour. Now the heavier weight of metal fired by the Yankee—684 pounds of iron balls from her broadside, against 556 pounds from *Guerrière*—and the sturdier construction of her hull, began to tell. A well-aimed ball brought down the Britisher's mizzenmast, the aftermost of her three masts, which plunged over the side into the water but was held against the hull by the rigging. This swung the ship around and permitted Captain Hull on *Constitution* to rake her first with the starboard battery, then by wearing round, or turning away from the wind, to rake her again with the port broadside.

However, Captain Hull crossed *Guerrière*'s bows so closely that her bowsprit caught in *Constitution*'s mizzen rigging and the two ships swung together. Both captains called for boarding parties, using the fouled bowsprit as a bridge, but the seas were so rough the idea was given up, although at such close range the muskets of the marines on both sides did appalling damage to both crews. Captain Dacres and Charles Morris, first lieutenant of *Constitution* were both wounded.

Some of *Guerrière*'s gunners managed to clear away fallen rigging and debris from the few guns still workable and sent several rounds into the stern of *Constitution*, setting fire to Hull's cabin, but the fire was soon put out and the ships drifted apart. The Yankee crew managed to patch up her rigging and *Constitution* bore down once more on the helpless Britisher, whose foremast and bowsprit had also fallen by now, but the Americans could see that *Guerrière*, rolling wildly in the troughs, was rapidly sinking.

Captain Hull sent over a boat and received Dacres' surrender; then both crews helped to transfer the wounded to *Constitution* without losing a man. *Guerrière* lost 78 of her crew of 272 in killed and wounded, almost 30 percent, while *Constitution*'s casualties amounted to only 3 percent of her crew of 456 men.

Captain Hull brought his ship back to Boston on August 30, 1812, and landed his prisoners in the midst of a wildly cheering crowd. It was a heartening event for Americans, after suffering several disasters earlier in this war at the hands of the British, and it came as a great shock to the British, who were accustomed only to victories by their navy, which had scorned American warships and the fighting abilities of American seamen.

Constitution was the outstanding fighting ship in the American sailing navy. She had been in action against the Tripolitan pirates in the Mediterranean in the early 1800's and, during the War of 1812, under several captains, she defeated a number of British frigates in hot engagements, for which she earned the nickname "Old Ironsides," and she took many prizes. She was never defeated in battle, and after an illustrious career now lies moored at the Charlestown Navy Yard in Boston harbor. Still in commission after several complete rebuildings, one of which was paid for by the pennies of American schoolchildren, her yards still crossing her sturdy masts and her batteries of 24-pounders and carronades still lining her gun deck, she is the oldest battleship still afloat.

Chapter 9

The triumph of *Constitution* was only one of a number of American naval victories. Two months later the American sloop *Wasp* came upon the British brig *Frolic*, a vessel of about the same size, escorting a convoy of merchantmen. After a half hour of furious broadsides, *Frolic* was dismasted and the American boarding party found almost her entire crew dead or wounded. Just as Captain Jacob Jones was about to put aboard a prize crew, the big British *Poictiers*, 74, came along and captured both ships, but Captain Jones could still feel he had won a clean victory.

On October 25, 1812, the frigate *United States*, with Stephen Decatur, hero of the Tripolitan war as captain, met the British frigate *Macedonian*, and after a ninety-minute battle, forced her to surrender and brought her into Newport as a prize.

December 29, 1812 saw another victory for the frigate *Constitution*, now commanded by Captain Bainbridge. He met the British frigate *Java*, under Captain Lambert, a skilled and experienced commander, off the coast of Brazil and, after an hour of maneuvering, the superior gunnery of the Americans battered *Java* so severely that her guns were silenced and she was set afire. Captain Lambert and many of his crew were killed. *Constitution* lost only a few men, but she was so heavily damaged that she had to return to the United States to refit.

On February 24, 1813, the sloop *Hornet*, *Wasp's* sister ship, which had accompanied *Constitution* on her Brazil cruise, met the British brig *Peacock*, of about the same size but with lighter armament. In the battle that followed, *Peacock* was sunk. James

Lawrence, captain of *Hornet*, rescued the crew and sailed *Hornet* safely back to New York.

This string of victories by the United States Navy over the "invincible" British navy was beginning to have its effect on the British public. After the loss of *Java*, "Pilot," a publication on naval affairs published in London, bitterly called attention to this, the third frigate that had struck to the Americans. It stated:

"This is an occurrence which calls for serious reflection. This,

Hornet defeats **Peacock**

and the fact stated in our paper yesterday, that Lloyd's [the insurance company] list contains notices of upwards of five hundred British vessels captured in seven months by the Americans. Yet down to the moment not a single American frigate has struck her flag. They insult and laugh at our want of enterprise and vigor. They leave their ports when they please and return to them when it suits their convenience; they traverse the Atlantic; they beset the West Indian Islands; they advance to the very chops [waves] of the Channel; they parade along the coasts of South America; nothing chases, nothing intercepts, nothing engages them but to yield them triumph."

The unexpected triumph of the tiny American navy over the mighty British fleet was not to last much longer. It had been possible up to this point only because England was still engaged in its desperate struggle with Napoleon.

By 1812 Napoleon was taking the first of the steps that would eventually lead to his downfall. They started with his invasion of Spain in March, 1808, which he undertook partly to drive the British from their ally Portugal and thus to close every European port to England. He was opposed by fierce bands of Spanish guerrillas, aided by a large British army under General Arthur Wellesley, later to become the famous Duke of Wellington. These allies inflicted such heavy losses on the French troops that Napoleon had to keep an army of three-hundred thousand men in Spain, which weakened his field forces across the Pyrenees.

The fierce fighting in Spain called for mountains of supplies and munitions for the British armies and their Portuguese and Spanish allies, all of which had to be shipped from England in convoys that had to be guarded by naval escorts from a fleet already overtaxed by all its other duties. This was why, in 1812, the British navy could only blockade Chesapeake and Delaware bays, leaving hundreds of miles of coastal ports and bays open to the passage of American warships, privateers, and merchantmen.

In the summer of 1812 Napoleon made the fatal mistake of his career: he declared war on Russia and, with his Grand Army of Frenchmen and his Prussian and Austrian allies five-hundred thousand strong, marched on Moscow, which he entered trium-

Napoleon at St. Helena

phantly on September 14. He found that the country had been swept clean of food for his men and fodder for the horses by the Russians, who finally even burned the city, leaving his army neither rations nor shelter. By October he was forced to retreat, harassed by continual Russian cossack cavalry attacks and by the even more brutal cold of the fierce Russian winter.

Only a sixth of his Grand Army ever returned; two-hundred fifty thousand of his veterans died or were captured, and he began for the first time to meet serious military reverses, which ended in the disastrous battle of Leipzig in October, 1813.

After that the end was inevitable. On April 12, 1814, Napoleon was forced to abdicate. He was permitted to retire to the island of Elba, in the Mediterranean, while France was once again put under the rule of a Bourbon, Louis XVIII, by the allies. Napoleon escaped from Elba, returned to France and, on March 1, 1815, entered Paris in triumph, once more the Emperor, while King Louis fled.

This time Napoleon's reign lasted only a hundred days; his army was totally defeated by Wellington and Blücher at Waterloo, and he was once again exiled, this time to a tiny lonely island in the middle of the South Pacific, called St. Helena, guarded, of course, by the British navy. There he died, a lonely, broken man, in 1821.

Chapter 10

What of the France Napoleon left behind? Paris and the other French cities were in a sad state of neglect and disrepair after the violence of the Revolution, the Commune, and finally the Empire, years when conscription had taken almost every able-bodied man into the army, while materials and labor were all devoted to military needs.

Streets were left unrepaired and unswept, roofs and walls leaked and crumbled, gates lay torn from their hinges. Drains and sewers were clogged and broken, and the water supply had become a serious problem for the cities. In Paris most people had to buy their water from the Auvergnat water peddlers—natives of the province of Auvergne who specialized in carting supplies. They trundled wooden water butts mounted on wheels, from which hung water buckets. These, filled with water, cost two sous each, and the water probably came from the nearby dirty, polluted Seine. Filthy drains ran down the middle of the streets, forcing pedestrians to hug the walls of the houses, where they had to dodge the piles of uncollected garbage.

In the early 1800's Paris was far from being the glamorous "City of Light" it became later. Here and there a dim lantern, swinging from the end of a rope, cast a feeble glow, unless it had been extinguished by wind or rain or left unlighted so that the lamplighter could sell the oil. The streets were so dark and full of holes that every night private lantern bearers gathered outside theaters and public buildings, hiring out to light their customers to their homes.

Police and postal services were disorganized, and there were

Lantern bearers guided theatergoers (note water cart lower right)

Paris roads were very bad

so few cabs and omnibuses it was almost impossible to go about the cities. The roads in the provinces were so bad that the drivers of the mail coaches often had to get out and walk to keep from having their necks broken, and luckless travelers along the roads also faced the danger of being robbed and killed by the swarms of penniless returned soldiers turned highwaymen.

Even worse was the food situation. Flour for bread became scarce because there were not enough farmers to raise wheat or millers to grind it; they had all been conscripted. Long lines of people stood before closed bakeries waiting, to find that many of them sold bread only "under the counter" for high prices, which often brought on fierce bread riots.

Conditions in England were bad, too. The interference with shipping, which brought trade with Europe and America almost to a standstill, plus the losses from captured ships and cargoes, put thousands out of work and bankrupted merchants, while the heavy cost of maintaining the army and navy meant high taxes for all. While life was not quite so bad as in France, the common people were beginning to demand peace.

Still, after Napoleon's fall, British troops could at last be brought home from Spain, and the fleet no longer had to blockade French ports, since France was now again under a king who was beholden to England. Now there were plenty of warships to send across the Atlantic to put those proud upstarts, the Yankees, in their places, and so, on March 30, 1813, the blockade of the American coast by British ships, under Admirals Cockburn and Warren, was extended from New York all down the coast. Six months later Long Island Sound was closed, as well as the harbors up the coast to Canada.

By May, 1813, the entire American coast was tightly blockaded. United States frigates lay idle, unable to get to sea, and American shipping was driven from the ocean. Even coastwise trade and fishing ceased, and merchandise destined for delivery between the coastal cities had to be carried in wagons over the wretched roads, at great delay and expense. A few blockade-runners and privateers, and an occasional warship slipped through in stormy weather, but most ships rotted at their piers.

After the blockade was clamped down, only two noteworthy encounters between British and American vessels took place. On June 1, 1813, Captain Broke, commanding the blockading frigate *Shannon* off Boston, sent Captain Lawrence commanding *Chesapeake*, lying in Boston harbor, a challenge to come out and fight. Although his crew was green and still untrained, Lawrence accepted the challenge and sailed out to do battle. In a fifteen-minute fight at close quarters the veteran crew of *Shannon* raked *Chesa-*

peake so severely that her crew quickly surrendered to a British boarding party, although the dying Captain Lawrence made his famous plea, "Don't give up the ship; blow her up."

One United States frigate, *Essex*, built at Salem, Massachusetts, with money contributed by the citizens of the town, made a historic voyage to the Pacific. In 1812 her commander, David Porter, had been ordered to rendezvous with *Constitution* and *Hornet* off Brazil on the cruise that resulted in *Constitution*'s defeat of *Java*. As so often happened in the days before steam and radio, Porter missed connections with his squadron and so finally decided to go it alone. He decided to round Cape Horn, cruise the Pacific, and try to snap up any British whalers he might find there. After surviving heavy winter storms off the Horn he finally made Valparaiso, Chile, where he refitted. From there he headed for the Galápagos Islands, where he captured three British whalers and two privateers, aboard which he placed American crews. Porter now commanded a squadron of six vessels mounting 80 guns, which he took to the Marquesas Islands in mid-Pacific, where he wintered.

In the spring of 1814, Captain Porter returned to Valparaiso in *Essex*, and learned that the British brig *Phoebe* and the sloop *Cherub* were looking for him. They soon appeared in the harbor but did not break the neutrality of the Chilean port, and presently they took station outside to blockade him. For six weeks, *Essex* lay in Valparaiso harbor but, when Porter learned that more enemy vessels were on the way, he decided to slip out and escape. Unluckily, a fierce sudden squall brought down his mainmast as he was running out of the harbor and he was forced to anchor just offshore. The two British ships, ignoring the neutrality which should have protected Porter within the three-mile limit, attacked his helpless vessel with their long guns from beyond the reach of his short-range carronades. After many of his crew became disabled, he struck his colors, which ended the last great sea battle of the war.

Although the defeat of *Essex* and the blockading of the American fleet in port by strong British squadrons marked the end of active naval affairs in 1814, a few American ships did manage to

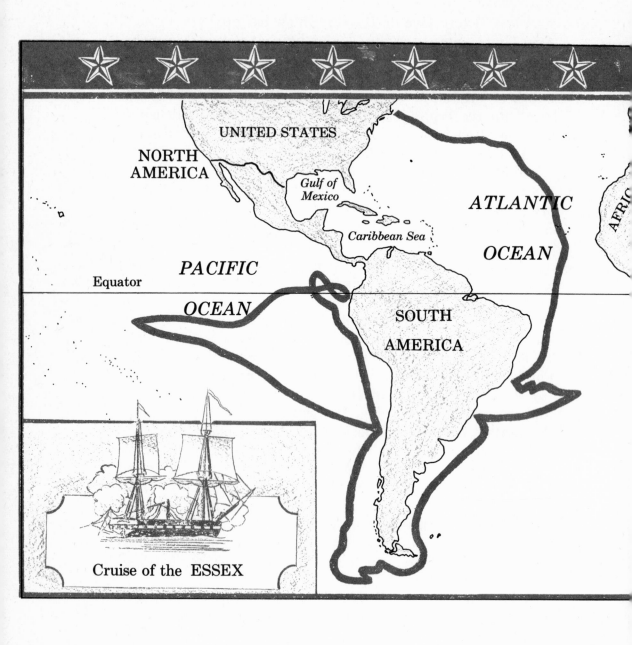

NORTH
AMERICA

UNITED STATES

Gulf of
Mexico

Caribbean Sea

PACIFIC

OCEAN

Equator

ATLANTIC

OCEAN

AFRIC

SOUTH

AMERICA

Cruise of the ESSEX

slip through the blockade to harry British shipping and defeat smaller naval vessels.

On January 14, 1815, Captain Decatur, now commanding the frigate *President*, slipped out of New York harbor during a heavy gale which blew the British blockading squadron off station. Unfortunately, the pilot lost his bearings in the storm and put the ship on the bar; she was badly strained in working off, and should have returned for docking, but the gale prevented her from returning, so she ran before it along the Long Island shore during the night. At dawn she was sighted by a British squadron of three frigates and a big razee (a 74 with upper deck cut down, reducing her size) which at once gave chase. The damage done to *President* when she grounded cut her speed and she was leaking, so presently *Endymion*, a fast-sailing frigate, overtook her and firing commenced, during which Decatur was wounded by a splinter that struck his head.

Finally *President*'s broadsides battered *Endymion*'s guns into silence and dismasted her, but by now the other three ships surrounded her and Decatur was forced to strike his flag.

Other blockade-runners were more fortunate. A week later, in another storm, the sloop *Hornet* also escaped and soon intercepted and burned several big Indiamen. Presently she encountered *H.M.S. Penguin* which was searching for a privateer for which she mistook *Hornet*. After a sharp exchange of broadsides, *Penguin* became a wreck, with her foremast over the side, and she was forced to strike.

On another occasion, the privateer *General Armstrong*, while at anchor in the neutral harbor of Fayal, in the Azores, was attacked by the boats of a three-ship British squadron, which was prevented by shoal water from approaching and getting in range. After a furious battle, during which the boarding party was repulsed with a loss of thirty-four British seamen killed and eighty-six wounded, the British sloop *Carnation* was towed within range by her boats and began cannonading the American. The crew of *Armstrong* finally scuttled her and rowed ashore safely.

The renowned and unbeatable *Constitution* also added another victory to her score. Under a new commander, Captain Stewart, she slipped out of Boston harbor during a winter gale and ran eastward toward the Mediterranean to do whatever damage she could. When the British blockaders learned that *Constitution* had slipped through their fingers, they sent word to London that "the devil was loose once more" and took after her with a battleship and three frigates, but she was too fast for them and was soon taking prizes off the coast of Spain.

Then Stewart sighted two sail, and by six in the evening found them to be the sloop *Levant* and the frigate *Cyane*. The battle began but *Constitution* was, as usual, too much for the British. Her sharp maneuvering and superior gunnery soon wrecked their gun carriages and made a shambles of their decks by well-aimed raking broadsides, so that by ten o'clock both ships surrendered.

The knowledge that no blockade seemed able to keep those formidable American frigates from getting loose and creating havoc among British shipping had a sobering effect on the government, and was one reason the Prince of Wales, acting as Regent for his father, insane King George III, finally agreed to appoint peace commissioners to meet with the Americans.

Chapter 11

While our frigates and privateers were giving such a good account of themselves at sea, the warfare on land in the North and West was not going so well. American military land forces were not much stronger than the navy in 1812. The United States Army consisted of only ten regiments of regulars which were at less than half their strength of one thousand men each, scattered in a number of small forts facing the Indian tribes on the frontier. There was one company manning a wooden stockade fort at Detroit, one company at another blockhouse fort at Mackinac, at the head of Lake Huron, and a half company at Fort Dearborn, the site of present-day Chicago. These were our only defenses in the West against the Indians.

The army was commanded by eight elderly, not very able generals, veterans of the Revolution, with General Wilkinson as its chief. Besides the regulars there were the untrained companies of the various state militia, who almost always ran away during a battle, and who later refused to cross the border into Canada to come to the aid of our regular troops who were being overwhelmed by the British. There were continuous quarrels between the states and the national government; the governors of Connecticut, Rhode Island, and Massachusetts even refused to send their militia to war at President Madison's call; 1812 was a Southern and Western war; New England was stubbornly against it.

In 1812, the boundary between Canada and the United States ran through the middle of the Great Lakes (except Lake Michigan), along the St. Lawrence River from the eastern end of Lake Ontario for some distance, and then around northern New

WIS.

MICH.

2

15

C A N A D A

13

11

9

8 10

7

3

4

6

N.Y.

5

1

ILL.

IND.

OHIO

PA.

The War on the Canadian Frontier

1. Fort Dearborn
2. Sault Ste. Marie
3. Detroit
4. Fort Malden
5. Put-in-Bay
6. Presque Isle
7. Fort Erie

8. Queenston
9. Fort George
10. Fort Niagara
11. York
12. Sackett's Harbor
13. Kingston
14. To Montreal

15. Mackinac

York, Vermont, New Hampshire, and Maine to the coast. Canada was a vast, almost uninhabited wilderness, with most of its French-speaking population living along the St. Lawrence, where its largest cities, Quebec and Montreal, lay. Its whole population, in 1812, was less than half a million. Westward, in what was then called Upper Canada, settlements of English-speaking colonists were spread in a thin layer, hugging the shores of the Great Lakes as far west as Malden, a fort at the mouth of the Detroit River on Lake Erie.

The Canadian border was defended by a fort at Malden, one at Kingston at the outlet of Lake Erie, and two more at each end of the Niagara River—Fort Erie and Fort George. At the extreme eastern end of the border, the Adirondack, Green, and White Mountains, and the trackless wilderness, made military operations almost impossible.

The United States War Department, believing that its chances were better on land against England than at sea, decided to send its main force up Lake Champlain, down the Richelieu River, and up the St. Lawrence to Montreal, while three other columns crossed the border at Detroit, Niagara, and Sackets Harbor, opposite Kingston. The American forces outnumbered the British, but their generals seemed to forget that the American troops were untrained militia who would seldom stand up and fight against regulars.

Meanwhile, William Hull, governor of the Michigan Territory—that vast wilderness west of the Great Lakes inhabited mostly by Indians—and uncle of the brilliant frigate captain, Isaac Hull, was to attack the western end of the frontier, cross the Detroit River, and capture Malden. Hull's side of the frontier was defended by a blockhouse at Mackinac, by Fort Dearborn—a log stockade at the foot of Lake Michigan—and by another fort at Detroit, guarding the straits.

In May, 1812, General Hull left southeastern Ohio with some three hundred regulars and eleven hundred militia, reaching Detroit on July 12, prepared to cross the river and attack Malden if necessary, but he had not yet been informed that the United States had actually declared war. With no thought of danger, he

Blockhouse fort at Mackinac

sent a schooner with all his plans and papers, his baggage, and some sick men up from Lake Erie on the way to Detroit, right past Malden, whose commander did know of the declaration of war; he intercepted and captured the schooner, thereby learning all the American war plans.

General Isaac Brock, the capable and energetic British commander at Malden, with a force of well-trained Canadian militia, prepared for Hull's attack and was able to drive him back across the river. Brock also ordered Captain Roberts, in command of the Canadian fort at Sault Ste. Marie, to capture the fort at Mackinac. With three hundred men, the captain surprised the American garrison, which had not yet heard of the declaration of war, and captured the fort, sending the garrison, under parole, down to Detroit, where they told Hull of the surrender and of the approach of a horde of bloodthirsty redskins under their great war chief Tecumseh.

The news so terrified General Hull that, when Brock appeared before Detroit with a force smaller than his, Hull raised a white flag and meekly surrendered, an action for which he was later court-martialed. On the day before this surrender, the garrison at Fort Dearborn evacuated its stockade at Hull's orders, and as soon as they were in the open, were fallen upon and slaughtered by a huge war party of Indians. Thus, in a few days, all of the American western territory had fallen into the hands of a British force of less than a thousand men plus their Indian allies.

Dismayed by the sharp setback in the West, the government at Washington put Major General Dearborn, another mediocre veteran of the Revolution, in charge of the main army, which was having great difficulty in recruiting men because the New England states flatly refused to cooperate.

At last, with sixty-eight thousand poorly trained men, but outnumbering the British by four to one, Dearborn attacked Queenston Heights, at the mouth of the Niagara River, and gained a foothold on the Canadian side. General Brock, the best officer on the British side, was killed while leading an assault against the Yankees, a heavy blow to the British. However, reinforcements from Fort George turned the tide and the American regulars were pinned against the riverbank, overpowered, and forced to surrender.

From across the river a large force of American militia watched the regulars being slaughtered and refused to set foot out of New York State boundaries to help them, claiming that they had no authority to leave the state. After the battle the militia went home, the American general resigned in disgust, and the Niagara offensive petered out.

In 1813, a new campaign under General Dearborn was planned, to capture York (now Toronto) and Kingston. Commodore Chauncey was sent with a large party of ship's carpenters and naval ratings to build ships at Sackets Harbor, in order to gain control of Lake Ontario. With command of the lake in American hands, Dearborn was able to cross over and capture York and Fort George, at the mouth of the Niagara River, but when he attacked Hamilton he was repulsed and retired to Fort George.

Further battles at both ends of Lake Erie were indecisive, and at last the government at Washington realized that to win a permanent victory in Upper Canada and to gain permanent control of Lake Erie, the United States would have to build enough warships to defeat the British flotilla based at Malden, commanded by Captain Barclay.

By the middle of 1813, fighting was transferred from Lake Ontario westward to Lake Erie. The British squadron under Captain Barclay held a slight edge over the Americans; to overcome this, Navy Captain Oliver Hazard Perry was sent, with a force of ship's carpenters from the coast, to build an American fleet on Lake Erie.

The keels of the new vessels were laid at Presque Isle (now Erie, Pennsylvania) where a bar across the harbor mouth protected the shipyard from raids by Barclay's ships. Perry's men built several strange-looking flimsy craft, using green timber, the only wood they could get, whose planks were fastened to the frames with hand-whittled treenails, or wooden pegs, because of the scarcity of nails and other metal.

Because the lake was so shallow, the ships' hulls had to be very shallow draft, and so were inclined to be top-heavy, always in danger of capsizing from the weight of the cannon on deck. Their guns, borrowed from the army as well as from naval arsenals, were hauled up from Pittsburgh, or from tidewater over wilderness trails on wagons or sledges, or on barges rowed up the rivers. Anchors, cordage, sails, and rigging, as well as ammunition and food all had to be dragged laboriously to Presque Isle in the same way.

The British, who were also building a large ship-rigged vessel, *Detroit*, at Malden, had even more trouble in getting supplies; they had to be brought all the way from Montreal.

By July, 1813, despite an unreliable militia garrison which was supposed to protect them, sickness, and lack of skilled workmen, seamen, and supplies, Perry managed to finish two brigs and several small schooners. Here a new problem arose: his ships, with all their guns aboard, would draw too much water to cross the bar into the lake. The guns would have to be removed until the ships were floated over the bar and then remounted in the open lake, where Barclay's guns might surprise them and blow them out of the water while they were unarmed.

Fortunately, just as the American ships were finished, Barclay's squadron, which had been watching Presque Isle closely for some time, sailed away to the west, and Perry at once got busy.

Perry's ships taken over the bar at Presque Isle by barges (camels)

He found that the ships, even without the guns, still grounded on the bar, so he had water-filled, half-sunken barges, called camels, lashed to the sides of the new hulls and then pumped out, raising them just enough so they could scrape across. While they lay helpless, with guns and ammunition being ferried out to them, Barclay's sails reappeared on the horizon. Had he struck then, he could have annihilated Perry's ships, but it looked to him as if the Americans were all prepared to fight his outnumbered flotilla, and so he sailed away, his golden opportunity lost forever.

Now Perry commanded the lake. His ships moved west to the Bass Islands, near Put-in-Bay, just across the lake from Malden, and from there they sallied forth to keep an eye on the British ships bottled up there. The Americans now could cut off all supplies to the British troops and sailors and their Indian allies at the western end of Lake Erie, and soon Barclay was forced to put them on half rations. He dared not come out and fight Perry until his new ship, *Detroit*, was finished and armed, so the workmen labored around the clock to get her ready before they all starved. At last, just as their flour was being scraped from the bottoms of the barrels, *Detroit* was rigged and armed, and on September 10, Barclay sailed out to do battle.

Perry's flagship, *Lawrence*—named after his friend, the commander of the ill-fated *Chesapeake*—carried a flag Perry had ordered made, a blue flag bearing Lawrence's last words, "Don't give up the ship." The second of the two new large ships was *Niagara*, commanded by Captain Elliott, whose handling of her came close to losing the coming battle. The third largest vessel was *Caledonia*, a British ship that had been captured by Elliott the autumn before. Besides these Perry had the schooners *Ariel*, *Scorpion*, *Somers*, *Tigress*, and *Porcupine* and the sloop *Trippe*. *Lawrence* and *Niagara* mounted 20 guns each; all the others carried no more than 4 and most of them only 1. Total armament was 54 guns.

Barclay had *Detroit*, 19 guns, *Queen Charlotte*, 17, the brig *Hunter*, 10, the schooners *Lady Prevost*, 13, *Chippewa*, 1, and the sloop *Little Belt*, 3, a total of 63 guns. In spite of its more numerous guns, the British squadron was considered to be about two-thirds as strong as the American.

As soon as Perry saw the approaching enemy, he set sail and

Perry's flag for flagship *Lawrence*

emerged from his anchorage in the Bass Islands to challenge the British in the famous battle of Put-in-Bay. The American line, headed by *Lawrence*, came in range of *Detroit*'s long guns before Perry's short-range carronades could fire, so *Lawrence* was badly battered before she could begin to reply to the enemy. For some reason, *Niagara* lagged far behind, so that *Queen Charlotte*, which she should have engaged, was able to concentrate on *Lawrence*, too.

Soon four-fifths of the *Lawrence* crew were killed or wounded and the ship was out of action, but before she struck her flag, Perry, carrying his "Don't give up the ship" flag, leaped into one of his small boats and had himself rowed to *Niagara*, still far astern. He took command, ordering Elliott to bring up the small schooners, while he trimmed sheets and, in the freshening breeze, bore down on the enemy.

Meanwhile the battered *Detroit* and *Queen Charlotte* had fouled each other's rigging, and *Hunter* and *Lady Prevost* were drifting to leeward. The undamaged *Niagara* raked the two fouled vessels with broadsides at close range from her double-shotted, murderous carronades and soon forced them to surrender. Many of

Niagara defeats *Detroit* and *Queen Charlotte* at Put-in-Bay

their crews were killed or wounded, among them Captain Barclay, who had to be carried below. *Lawrence* was recaptured, and all of the smaller British ships were taken. The British squadron was annihilated, and Perry reported tersely to Washington: "We have met the enemy and they are ours."

As soon as word of the victory reached the American army under General William Henry Harrison, he had his troops ferried across the lake to attack Malden, but he found that British General Proctor was already retreating eastward along the Thames River in Canada. Proctor was overtaken and defeated in the battle of the Thames, during which the great war chief of the Indian tribes, Tecumseh, the implacable enemy of the United States, was killed. With Perry's victory, Lake Erie was firmly in American hands, Detroit was recaptured, every Briton had been driven from American soil, and an American army was established in Canada.

However, the British still held on to the isthmus and the river at Niagara which flowed from Lake Erie to Lake Ontario. General Jacob Brown, a fine regular officer, was ordered from French Mills to Sackets Harbor, but there found Commodore Chauncey's fleet bottled up by a superior British force, so he decided to march to Niagara and see what he could accomplish from that end of the lake.

On July 3, 1814, Brown crossed the river and captured Fort Erie without a fight, continued down the river and, two days later, won another battle at Chippewa. If he could now take Fort George at the mouth of the river he could control the entire isthmus, but for that operation he needed the help of Chauncey's fleet to engage the British ships.

Chauncey never came out of Sackets Harbor, and the British were thus able to bring up reinforcements on Lake Ontario and land an army under General Drummond. The two forces met at the battle of Lundy's Lane, only a mile behind Niagara Falls, in a bitter struggle which lasted through the afternoon and well into the night. It was a drawn battle, and the exhausted Americans returned to Fort Erie. Later they blew up the fort and retired into winter quarters on their side of the river, ending all hostilities on the entire Niagara frontier.

Chapter 12

Because, after Napoleon's surrender, the British government had ships released from blockading French harbors and veteran troops from the Duke of Wellington's army in Spain to spare, Parliament resolved to put a quick end to the defiant, upstart Yankees. It was to be a two-pronged attack: one, by sea, along the American coast; the other, a drive southward from Canada. British troops from Canada were to strike southward from Niagara, sweeping the Americans from the Great Lakes, and from Montreal, down the Hudson Valley to New York, by way of Lake Champlain, following the ill-fated route of General Burgoyne during the Revolution some thirty years before.

The new campaign opened in July, 1814, in Maine, with the capture of Moose Island and with an expedition up Penobscot Bay to the town of Castine. The garrison there blew up the fort and retreated. The British commander then sent an expedition thirty miles up the Penobscot River to capture the American frigate *Adams* anchored there, but her captain blew her up, too, and the British returned to their ships empty-handed except for what loot they could find in the houses of the nearby Maine villages.

Next, Commodore Sir Thomas Hardy was ordered to attack several towns along the Massachusetts, Rhode Island, and Connecticut coast. On August 9, four British ships felt their way cautiously in between Fishers Island and Watch Hill, anchored off the little town of Stonington, Connecticut, and began a two-day bombardment. Hardy sent in several armed barges and a launch filled with marines to make a landing on the west side of the point where the town lay, but they were driven off with heavy losses by the

Americans who swept the boats with canister from their three cannon—two 18-pounders and a 6-pounder.

The British tried again, this time on the east side of the point, but the militia had dragged their guns across to that side and were waiting to repulse them again. A number of houses were damaged by the British bombardment, but Sir Thomas had to sail away, unsuccessful, on August 12, with a loss of twenty-one killed and over fifty wounded.

Now the British were ready for larger operations. A large fleet, including transports carrying several thousand veteran troops, was sent to Bermuda, which was to be the staging area for attacks along the coast and a base for the blockading squadrons.

Meanwhile, the Duke of Wellington, commander in chief in England, named General Robert Ross, a vigorous and capable general, to head an expedition of thirty-five hundred of the finest men of his regiments, which sailed from Bordeaux, France, for Chesapeake Bay, where they were reinforced by a thousand marines from Admiral Cockburn's fleet. The troops landed at Benedict, forty miles southeast of Washington, from forty transports, over four thousand strong, and marched slowly inland in the stifling midsummer weather of 1814.

At Bladensburg, Maryland, on August 24, 1814, American General William Winder deployed his men across the road to Washington, where he determined to make a stand. President Madison, Secretary of State Monroe, and General Armstrong, the Secretary of War, drove down from the capital to inspect the defenses themselves but, after interfering with General Winder's placing of his troops, they departed before any shooting began.

As soon as the British appeared, fierce fighting broke out; before the battle was over the Americans lost 10 killed and 40 wounded, and the militia, five thousand strong, retreated in panic, forcing the cannoneers of Commodore Barney, of the navy, who had fought stubbornly and well, to fall back also. Thereupon the British marched without any resistance into Washington so quickly that their officers ate the meal which had just been prepared at the White House for the fleeing President. Mrs. Madison barely had time to cut from its frame a portrait of General Wash-

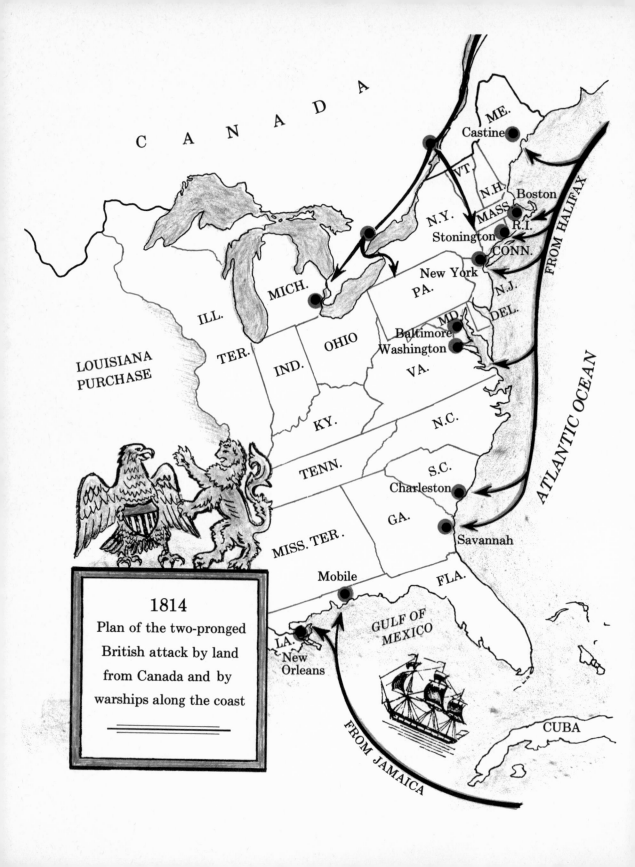

C A N A D A

ME.

Castine

VT

N.H.

Boston

N.Y.   MASS.

Stonington   R.I.

CONN.

New York   N.J.

MICH.   PA.

ILL.   MD.   DEL.

TER.   OHIO   Baltimore

IND.   Washington

VA.

LOUISIANA
PURCHASE

KY.   N.C.

TENN.   S.C.

Charleston

GA.

MISS. TER.   Savannah

Mobile   FLA.

GULF OF
MEXICO

LA.

New
Orleans

CUBA

ATLANTIC OCEAN

FROM HALIFAX

FROM JAMAICA

1814
Plan of the two-pronged
British attack by land
from Canada and by
warships along the coast

The burning of the White House

ington, roll it up along with the original draft of the Declaration of Independence, and escape with them in her coach.

General Ross then methodically set about burning the Capitol, the White House, and many other public buildings, while the troops looted private homes in reprisal, they claimed, for the treatment of York, in Canada, earlier by the Americans.

The British public, comparing it with London, believed that Washington was the most important American city. Feeling sure that this was a blow which would be hard for the United States to survive, they joyously celebrated their victory. Actually, although

Washington *was* the American capital, it was otherwise not very important, being still only a raw, straggling small town, twelve years old, with only eight thousand inhabitants.

During the night of August 25, General Ross, fearing an attack by gathering American forces, silently withdrew from the burning city and reembarked at Benedict. Within a few days the government returned to the city, moved into makeshift quarters for a time, and continued their duties.

However, the British fleet still lay in Chesapeake Bay and the Americans felt sure that Baltimore, near the head of the bay, the largest city in the area, was marked as the next victim. The people of the city hastily strengthened the fortifications on the landward side and manned them with five thousand militiamen.

On August 30, a landing party of two-hundred fifty men from the frigate *Menelaus*, headed by her captain, Sir Peter Parker, had come ashore at Moorfield on the eastern shore, across the bay from Baltimore, but were met by Maryland volunteers and driven back to their boats with a loss of thirty-five men killed or wounded, including Sir Peter, who died aboard his ship later.

Next, on September 11, General Ross, at the head of a force of eight thousand men, landed at North Point, twelve miles below Baltimore, from a fleet of forty vessels, and marched toward the city. Soon they made contact with American General Stricker's thirty-two hundred advance force, strengthened by six cannon and a cavalry detachment. General Ross attacked at once, leading his advance guard, and was promptly shot dead by an American sharpshooter.

The main British force then drove the volunteers back to their main line where a brisk fight ensued, and from which the outnumbered Americans retreated to their main defenses just outside the city. From there they could not be dislodged, and so, finding the nut too hard to crack, the British retreated during the night to their transports, with a loss of 290 men killed and wounded.

Meantime, sixteen British warships up-anchored and ran up the bay, although they could not get very close to the city itself because of shoal water. However, Fort McHenry was well within their range, and it became the target for a twenty-four hour bombardment of shells and Congreve rockets (an early type of rocket invented by an English officer of that name, which was fired from metal-lined tubes projecting from the sides of a bomb ship). The batteries of the fort replied vigorously whenever a British ship tried to approach; the fort's guns sank some and drove the others back.

A landing sortie in force above the fort, in armed boats from the fleet, was also repulsed by strong artillery fire, which caused heavy losses to the British and finally drove them back to the ships. This was Admiral Cockburn's last attempt to take the city; a few hours later the fleet weighed anchor and dropped down the bay, leaving Baltimore unconquered.

The gallant resistance of Fort McHenry achieved undying fame because a young American, who had gone out to the fleet under a flag of truce to try to get parole for a captured friend imprisoned on a ship, was detained aboard that night, and so he witnessed the furious all-night bombardment of the fort. The young man's name was Francis Scott Key, and what he saw that night inspired him to write a song which was to become our national anthem, *The Star-Spangled Banner*.

By now, Americans all along the seaboard were becoming discouraged by the successful blockade of the coast, by the burning of the capital city, Washington, and by the threat of still further attacks like the one at Baltimore. New Englanders felt that they had been pushed into a war by the West and the South, and now they had to bear the brunt of taxation and the ruin of their shipping, while the federal government seemed totally incapable of protecting their states from British raids.

In December, 1814, a convention of delegates from Massachusetts, Rhode Island, and Connecticut was held at Hartford to decide whether to make a separate peace with England and to secede from the United States before the West did, if England should win. Secession was defeated by the moderates and the convention merely signed a resolution condemning President Madison's handling of the war.

Chapter 13

While the British were carrying out the first part of their over-all plan by attacking the cities along the coast, General Sir George Prevost assembled an army in Canada to strike south. Although the Americans knew the vital importance of defending Lake Champlain, over which Prevost would have to ferry his troops southward, little had been done to fortify it. As early as June, 1813, British land forces had captured two of the three American sloops on the lake, when contrary winds had driven them under the guns of British land artillery. With these ships they controlled and ranged the length of the lake at will, destroying American barracks and stores on both banks.

To counter this, Commodore Thomas Macdonough, USN, had been put in charge of American naval operations on Lake Champlain, and he at once established a base and a shipyard far up a narrow channel at Otter Creek on the lake, which could be protected from the British sloops by some well-placed land guns.

In any gun duel between warships and land-based batteries, the advantage was always on the side of the land artillery, which could be shielded by stone, wooden, or earthwork ramparts. Sailing warships, on the other hand, were terribly vulnerable to missiles, which could splinter and smash the wooden hulls, bring down masts and rigging, and start devastating fires with hot shot, so naval commanders always tried to keep well clear of strong shore batteries.

At Otter Creek, in April, 1814, Macdonough had built and launched the 26-gun ship *Saratoga* and the 20-gun *Eagle*, and had altered a steamer into the 14-gun *Ticonderoga*. Besides these he had

Preble, 7, and a number of one-gun oared boats. His fleet was armed with whatever guns he could beg or borrow from Commodore Chauncey at Sackets Harbor and from the navy yards at Boston and New York.

On August 25, while the smoke of burning Washington was still darkening the air, the British launched the frigate *Confiance* at the head of Lake Champlain. Construction had been rushed on this 37-gun vessel in order to combat Macdonough's squadron. Though the British felt sure that their new *Confiance* could destroy the American squadron single-handed, Captain George Downie, R.N., in command, also had three smaller ships, *Finch, Linnet,* and *Chubb,* as well as some small armed boats.

On September 6, when Sir George Prevost received word that *Confiance* was afloat, he alerted his army of seven thousand British regulars, which lay before Plattsburg. The fort was defended by a brilliant American general, Alexander Macomb, with a much smaller force, but he threw up earthworks, mounted batteries of artillery, and disposed his men in strong positions, ready for a siege or an assault.

Prevost was in a hurry: he ordered Downie to attack the American ships at once, although *Confiance* was not yet fully prepared for action. Confident that Downie could defeat the American ships, he felt that, with their fleet destroyed, the discouraged Americans would soon give up. With the lake cleared and Macomb's armed resistance crushed, he could speedily march down the Hudson and take New York from the rear.

When the threat of an attack on Plattsburg seemed certain, Macdonough had sailed his squadron into Plattsburg Bay and anchored below the fort in a north-south line, with his biggest, *Eagle* and *Saratoga,* at the windward end. Being a careful and thorough officer, he had spring lines bent on to his anchor cables, which could be hauled in or slackened to swing his vessels while at anchor, but he also laid out kedge anchors from the bows forward, by which the ships could be completely turned around. This could be of enormous importance to a sailing warship, which carried its batteries in two broadsides, one on each side. If the one facing the enemy was disabled by his fire, the ship could be swung around to bring the undamaged broadside to bear. This foresight was to save the day for the Americans.

On the morning of September 11, the battle began. As Captain Downie's squadron rounded Cumberland Head and headed southward, close-hauled, to engage the Americans, the two squadrons were almost evenly matched in men and guns—four large ships and twelve gunboats against four large ships and ten gunboats.

When they came within range, Downie anchored *Confiance* and opened fire on *Saratoga* and *Eagle*, aided by *Linnet*, causing heavy damage aboard the American ships, but the double-shotted carronades of *Saratoga* made a shambles of the British flagship's decks and also cut one of her anchor cables. During the first deadly fifteen minutes Captain Downie was killed, a loss which was soon felt by the British.

The long guns of *Confiance* dismantled all the guns of *Saratoga*'s starboard battery and silenced her, but now Macdonough's forethought paid off. The wounded commander ordered his crew to tail onto the lines laid out to the kedges and *Saratoga* swung slowly around to present her undamaged port broadside to bear on the enemy. *Confiance* tried to follow suit, but she had no kedges out and the spring line on her remaining uncut anchor cable was not enough to turn her clear around. *Saratoga* was able to rake her until she had to surrender in a sinking condition, as did *Linnet* soon afterward.

Chubb had been captured and *Finch* drifted aground while the British small gunboats retreated rapidly up the lake. The American victory was complete, and Lake Champlain would now remain permanently in American hands.

General Prevost was shocked and dismayed by the defeat of his fleet and, after one feeble attack on the fort, he marched back to Canada that night. The British plan for an invasion from the north, which might have isolated New England from the rest of the country, was knocked into a cocked hat.

The American triumphs at Plattsburg and Baltimore had two important results. They heartened the discouraged American people, and gave the government some bargaining power in its peace negotiations with England, for by now peace feelers were being put out. England too was becoming concerned about peace: the ten percent tax levied on every Englishman to pay for the long Napoleonic wars was being continued because of the high cost of fighting in America, and the huge shipping losses due to the raids by American privateers still continued despite the British blockade.

As early as January, 1814, the British government had agreed to send representatives to meet with American commissioners to discuss the terms for peace. At first the British demanded control of the Great Lakes and the creation of a buffer state between the United States and Canada in the west, which would be a neutral territory belonging to the Indian tribes. This the Americans firmly refused, knowing that such a scheme would never work. Furthermore, the British refused to discuss the impressment of sailors or the blockading of American merchantmen, the actual causes of the war. However, months later, after the British defeats at Baltimore and Plattsburgh, and the Duke of Wellington's firm statement that England could never win without naval control of the Great Lakes, which she could now never hope to get, the British commissioners were more willing to compromise.

Finally both sides agreed to leave the long boundary between Canada and the United States unchanged, and to abandon the idea of an Indian buffer state. Impressment and blockading were not even mentioned in the treaty, and the Americans gave in on this; actually the British navy abandoned impressment forever after the Napoleonic wars and never again stopped and boarded American ships.

The commissioners met at Ghent, Belgium, the American side consisting of John Quincy Adams, James A. Bayard, Henry Clay, Jonathan Russell, and Albert Gallatin. The peace treaty was finally signed on Christmas Eve, December 24, 1814, but the document, which still had to be ratified by Congress and which was sent to New York aboard H.M.S. *Favorite*, was delayed seven weeks by howling westerly gales. When at last *Favorite* reached New York, fast relays of galloping horses carried the treaty to Washington, where the President signed it, and the Senate ratified it at once. The official date on which peace began was February 17, 1815, but the long delay in getting the treaty from Ghent to Washington brought about one of the most tragic events in civilized warfare.

Chapter 14

During the summer of 1814, Admiral Cochrane had been in command of the British blockading fleet, harassing the American coast. He had already taken and burned Washington and bombarded Baltimore; next he tried to start a revolt of the Negro slaves in Georgia. Then he attempted to arm the Creek and Choctaw Indians of the Southeast, so that they might attack Baton Rouge on the Mississippi and then take New Orleans from the rear. These plans came to nothing because a new American general, Andrew Jackson, was campaigning so vigorously in the Southeast that the Indians were afraid to go on the warpath without the backing of a large British army.

Cochrane then planned an attack along the Georgia coast as well as one against his main objective, New Orleans. By this time war again seemed likely in Europe, and the British government refused to send Cochrane as many troops as he wanted. The Admiral abandoned his foray on Georgia and began gathering his forces at Jamaica for the big attack on New Orleans. The Duke of Wellington sent his brother-in-law, Major General Sir Edward Pakenham, as commander of the ground troops, although the Duke was not much impressed by the abilities of Sir Edward.

Early in December, 1814, the expedition set sail from Jamaica. Cochrane had a choice of going up the Mississippi from its mouth, or from the gulf into Lake Borgne. The nearer way to the city by the river was blocked by Fort St. Philip, some miles below the city, so the Admiral chose the undefended Lake Borgne route and, on December 8, his warships and transports were anchored off Ship Island, seventy miles east of New Orleans. From there his

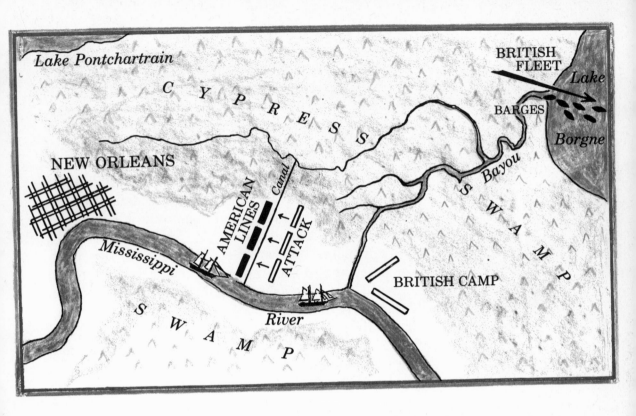

troops would have to be transported by the ships' launches across the shallow lake and through the streams which ran through swamps, before they could reach the firm banks of the Mississippi.

The way was disputed only by five of those previously useless gunboats President Jefferson had ordered built years before. They were commanded by Lieutenant Jones and they proved far from useless now. Though small, they were the largest craft in those swampy bayous, and Jones fought so well that Admiral Cochrane finally had to send as many as forty large, heavily armed launches before the American gunboats were captured, and then only after they had inflicted heavy losses on the British boats' crews and delayed their advance for six precious days. This gave Jackson time to collect his own scattered forces and throw up defenses.

The British had other troubles too: there were not enough small boats to carry all the troops at once, so the first contingent had to be ferried to an island in the lake, where it was disembarked to wait in the freezing rain and mud of the alligator-infested swamps while the boats went back to the fleet for another load.

It was not until Christmas Day, the day after the peace treaty had been signed in Ghent, that all the troops were rowed out of the swamps, and they pitched camp eight miles below New Orleans, where General Pakenham finally joined his command.

Meanwhile Andrew Jackson had been furiously busy. His troops had been scattered along the coast to fight off possible British attacks on Mobile and Pensacola, and upriver to defend Baton Rouge. The British delays gave him time to assemble his men and build fortifications at New Orleans. His main line, made partly of palmetto logs, cotton bales, and earth, stretching from the north bank of the river eastward to the impassable swamps, lay behind a canal, just below the city. It was manned by a mixed force of determined, well-trained regulars, buckskin-clad sharpshooting backwoodsmen with deadly rifles, local militia, and even a loyal band of picturesque smugglers and pirates from Barataria, in sashes and gold earrings, under Jean Lafitte. These men were good soldiers, many of them crack shots, and their line was well bolstered with cannon.

On the twenty-third, when only twenty-four hundred British troops had reached the river, Jackson attacked them. Two of his naval vessels, the schooners *Carolina* and *Louisiana*, came down the river and opened fire on the British camp, bringing down a number of troopers who had no shelter, while Jackson's men for three hours fought a bloody hand-to-hand engagement, during which hundreds on both sides were killed or wounded, before the Americans retired to their lines.

When Pakenham arrived with the remainder of his army, he found the troops already there encamped on a narrow strip of level land between the river and the swamps, unprotected from the fire of the two schooners on the river. He at once had heavy guns and a hot-shot furnace brought up and, with red-hot cannon balls, soon drove *Louisiana* back upriver and set *Carolina* afire.

After a preliminary attack which was repulsed by the Americans, Pakenham brought up more heavy guns from the fleet, and

Battle of New Orleans

both sides cannonaded each other's lines, demolishing the make-shift British parapets built of sugar hogsheads, and setting fire to the American cotton-bale walls.

Then for a week the British troops dug a canal from Lake Borgne to the Mississippi and floated over some of the fleet's boats, which ferried a battalion of infantry across the river to attack the Americans stationed on the south bank, while the main force stormed Jackson's lines frontally. At dawn on the eighth of January, the British grenadiers, their red coats in a ruler-straight line, marched steadily to their deaths. Although the peace treaty had been signed two weeks before, nobody on either side knew anything about it, and the battle began.

The British attackers were to have been preceded by an Irish and a colored regiment, carrying bundles of brush to fill the canal and scaling ladders to mount the breastworks. Somehow they failed to do their duty, and when the British infantry arrived they found it almost impossible to cross and make the assault. In close ranks in the open, they faced the Americans' cannon belching flame and deadly showers of canister, and the sharp cracking of the frontiersmen's deadly rifles, and their line melted away into sprawling heaps.

Within twenty-five minutes Generals Pakenham and Gibbs were killed and General Keane was seriously wounded; seven hundred of the infantry lost their lives and fourteen hundred were wounded, while five hundred were taken prisoner. The Americans lost only six killed; it was a complete and devastating British defeat.

The next day, during an armistice, the two armies buried their dead and attended their wounded, after which the British began an orderly retreat and withdrawal, without interference by the Americans, and on the eighteenth of January they sailed away. On their way home they entered the mouth of the Mississippi and engaged Fort St. Philip, but without success. Then, on the coast east of the river, they stormed and captured Fort Bowyer, on the very day that H.M.S. *Favorite* passed Sandy Hook and entered New York harbor with the peace treaty.

Chapter 15

The uneasy peace in Europe, after Napoleon's fall, lasted for forty years, until the outbreak of the Crimean War. The warships of Britain policed the rest of the world, and the United States was left free to rebuild its shattered economy during its thirty years of peace between 1815 and the war with Mexico in 1846.

The South grew prosperous with the rise in importance of King Cotton, while New England became a land of smoking factory and mill chimneys, where the Yankees put their energies to manufacturing and to rebuilding the almost destroyed merchant marine. New York and Boston saw the rise of that queen of the seas, the clipper ship, which would dominate the sea routes and bring prosperity to ship owners for a few short years until the steamship crowded it out.

The most spectacular changes were happening in the West. In 1800 the frontier that divided the country settled by white farmers from the wilderness inhabited only by Indian tribes and a few trappers, still lay to the east of the Appalachians. It ran through present-day Vermont, New York, Pennsylvania, and western Virginia, skirted North Carolina and passed through the middle of Georgia to the northern boundary of Spanish Florida.

Spain still controlled the Southwest from Texas to the Pacific, including California, which the Spanish had occupied formally in 1769, and where Father Junípero Serra had built a string of nine missions, from San Diego to San Francisco. Spain also again held Florida, returned to her by England, which she had once desperately needed to prevent English or French pirates and privateers

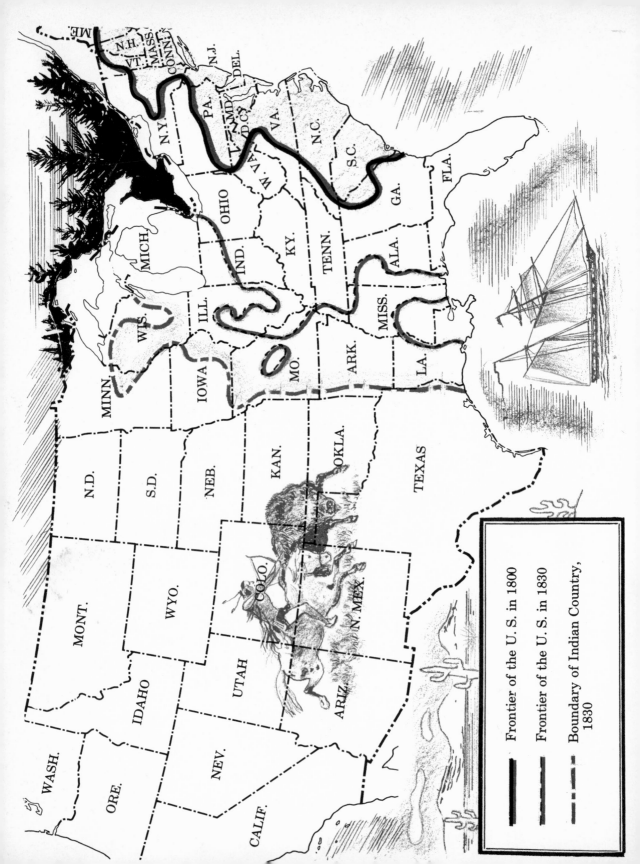

Frontier of the U. S. in 1800

Frontier of the U. S. in 1830

Boundary of Indian Country, 1830

from using it as a base from which to attack and plunder her fleets of treasure galleons passing along the Florida coast in the Gulf Stream on the way from Mexico to Cadiz. Since there were no more fleets of treasure galleons plying the Spanish Main by 1819, Florida was no longer of any use to Spain, so she sold it to the United States.

Later, in the 1840's, Texas, Utah, Nevada, Arizona, and California were acquired by the United States by annexation, conquest and purchase. Then, at last, the United States flag floated over the entire land, from the eastern seaboard to the Pacific coast, from the Great Lakes and the 49th parallel (the Canadian border) to the Rio Grande on the south.

The population had grown from 1,600,000 in 1763 to 5,308,000 in 1800. After that it swelled so fast through immigration from Europe that by 1830 the frontier had been pushed to the banks of the Mississippi. The native Indians were being driven farther and farther west to new reservations, which were soon overrun by new floods of white settlers. By 1850 the tide of immigration had reached Oregon and California, on the Pacific coast.

Mexico and South America, except for Portuguese Brazil, were still colonies of Spain at the beginning of the nineteenth century, but in 1821 Venezuelan revolutionists, headed by Simón Bolívar, declared their independence, and soon the other Spanish colonies followed Venezuela to independence.

Spain called for help from the Holy Alliance, which included Russia, Austria, and Prussia, but when it looked as though some European nation might try to interfere in the affairs of the newly freed South American colonies, President Monroe, in his message to Congress on December 2, 1823, put into words the famous Monroe Doctrine which stated that any attempt by a non-American power to colonize in the American continent or interfere with any nation on the face of it, would be considered by the United States to be a hostile act. Except for a brief French occupation of Mexico during our Civil War, during which the French troops were hastily withdrawn when they were threatened by the huge Union army, the American continent has ever since remained free of interference by overseas powers.

INDEX

[94]